The Art of Kindness

THE Art OF Kindness

Relating More Deeply with
Self, Others, and God

100 Journeys in Spiritual Wellness

Robert J. Wicks

Paulist Press
New York / Mahwah, NJ

Unless otherwise stated, Scripture quotations are from New Revised Standard Version Bible: Catholic Edition, copyright © 1989, 1993 National Council of the Churches of Christ in the United States of America. Used by permission. All rights reserved worldwide.

Cover image by Dimitri Tymchenko/Shutterstock.com
Cover and book design by Lynn Else

Copyright © 2025 by Robert J. Wicks

All rights reserved. No part of this publication may be reproduced, stored in a retrieval system, or transmitted in any form or by any means, electronic, mechanical, photocopying, recording, scanning, or otherwise, without either the prior written permission of the Publisher, or authorization through payment of the appropriate per-copy fee to the Copyright Clearance Center, Inc., www.copyright.com. Requests to the Publisher for permission should be addressed to the Permissions Department, Paulist Press, permissions@paulistpress.com.

Library of Congress Cataloging-in-Publication Data
Names: Wicks, Robert J., author.
Title: The art of kindness: relating more deeply with self, others, and God / Robert J. Wicks.
Description: New York, Mahwah, NJ: Paulist Press, [2025] | Summary: "This book presents one hundred reflections on ways that we can relate better with self, others, and God"—Provided by publisher.
Identifiers: LCCN 2024028796 (print) | LCCN 2024028797 (ebook) | ISBN 9780809157266 (paperback) | ISBN 9780809188949 (ebook)
Subjects: LCSH: Kindness—Religious aspects—Christianity.
Classification: LCC BV4647.K5 W43 2025 (print) | LCC BV4647.K5 (ebook) | DDC 241/.4—dc23/eng/20241125
LC record available at https://lccn.loc.gov/2024028796
LC ebook record available at https://lccn.loc.gov/2024028797

ISBN 978-0-8091-5726-6 (paperback)
ISBN 978-0-8091-8894-9 (ebook)

Published by Paulist Press
997 Macarthur Boulevard
Mahwah, NJ 07430
www.paulistpress.com

Printed and bound in the
United States of America

Dedication
*For the Sisters, Servants of the Immaculate Heart of Mary,
who live and minister at Camilla Hall,
in gratitude for their collective wisdom, witness to faith,
and life of prayer that blesses us all.*

When a flower doesn't bloom, you fix the environment in which it grows, not the flower.

~ Alexander den Heijer

Contents

Preface xiii

Introduction: Navigating the Road Ahead xv

1. We Are Not Alone 1
2. Refreshing Spiritual Rivers 3
3. Psychology and Faith 5
4. Tears of Joy 7
5. The Gift of Prayer 9
6. Quiet Despair 11
7. A New Life Now 13
8. A Grace from God 15
9. Finding Clarity 16
10. The Spirit of Intrigue 18
11. The Circle of Grace 20
12. A New Voice 22
13. Your Goodness Will Not Be Lost 23
14. Spiritual Mindfulness 25
15. The Virtue of Ordinariness 26
16. Peace versus Boredom 27

CONTENTS

17. The Presence of Wonder 28
18. The Birthday Lesson 30
19. Gratitude, Graciousness, and Intrigue 32
20. Memories 34
21. The Evidence of Pure Grace 36
22. Learn to Rest, Not to Quit 38
23. Meditation 39
24. A *Mitzvah* 40
25. Are We Listening? 41
26. An Amazing Meeting 42
27. Those Wonderful Scents 43
28. You Decide! 45
29. Making Wonderful Ideals a Reality 47
30. New Spiritual Wisdom 49
31. The Two Roads 51
32. Enjoy the Moment 52
33. Your Quiet History 53
34. A Rich, Compassionate, and Meaningful Life 54
35. Let Go! 56
36. Faithfulness 58
37. Dealing with Negativity 60
38. Stimulus and Response 62
39. The Basic Elements of Friendship 63

Contents

40. The Hidden Intentions 65
41. Your Own Karma 67
42. The Faithfulness Business 69
43. Appreciation of Others 71
44. Personal Limits 72
45. The Cost of Presence 74
46. The Beauty of Compassion 76
47. While the World Goes On 78
48. Pause before Responding 80
49. Enriching Our Interior Life 82
50. The Difficult Book 84
51. Hold On! 86
52. Actively Loving Oneself and Others 87
53. Loneliness 89
54. Caring for the Caregiver 91
55. The "Cana Effect" 93
56. Feeling Lost 95
57. Lifting the Heavy Bales 96
58. Tears of Renewed Wisdom 97
59. A Difference Is Possible 100
60. Stumbling on God's Love 103
61. See the Gifts 104
62. The Gift of Spiritual Sadness 105

CONTENTS

63. A Loved, Imperfect Disciple 107
64. Defending the Defenseless 108
65. Your Special Day 110
66. Resignation and Acceptance 111
67. Our Soft Spots 112
68. A Painful Journey 113
69. Spiritual and Psychological Carbon Monoxide Poisoning 115
70. The Challenge of Transition 118
71. Our Gifts and Growth 120
72. Meditative Moments 122
73. The Circle of Grace 123
74. God's Emanating Love 124
75. A Gentle Presence 125
76. The Ripple Effect 126
77. Memorial Day 128
78. Openness and Compassion 130
79. Holy Selfishness 132
80. Silence and Solitude 133
81. Invisible Connections 134
82. Seeing More Clearly 136
83. Walking Gently Together 137
84. Embracing Impermanence 138
85. Two Different Women 141

Contents

86. Some Life Lessons	143
87. Faith and Respect	146
88. Healing	148
89. Listening	149
90. Different Beautiful Gifts	150
91. The Lighthouse	151
92. Positive Prophets	153
93. The Gifts of Clarity	155
94. Good Friendship	157
95. Enjoying Life	158
96. Humility	160
97. The Countryside of Compassion	162
98. Invisible Darkness	164
99. Our Hidden Mental Compartments	166
100. Powerful Spaces	167
About the Author	169
Other Books by Robert J. Wicks	171
Praise for Other Books	173

*~ Rest can cure people who are physically exhausted.
But when they are psychologically
and spiritually depleted they need something more...
something different. ~*

Preface

Many people who consult with me as a therapist, mentor, clinical supervisor, or guide are not necessarily physically exhausted—rest can cure that—they are actually *psychologically and spiritually depleted*. In addition to the continual negative news on the internet and television, the burdens of their own personal and professional responsibilities keep draining their spirit. The result is a vague feeling of hopelessness that is only occasionally interrupted by uplift.

Spiritual refreshment is needed by all of us if we are to live our lives and share them more fully with others. Consequently, there are some initial steps that can be taken to care for our inner lives. For instance, all of us should practice simple nourishing activities, such as:

- Spending at least a few moments each day in silence and solitude—not to brood over life but to breathe in deeply a sense of being one with the beauty of this world in a unitive way.
- Sharing conversations and experiences with positive friends who reflect the loving face of God and the natural gifts of the world.
- Ceasing to speak negatively about public figures or people we know personally because, rather than giving us hope and freedom, this often contaminates our spirits. (If "psychological acid" comes out of our mouths, then our own mouths will be burned by it.)

THE ART OF KINDNESS

- Taking short walks in the morning or evening to provide oxygen that will physically support our efforts at spiritual refreshment.
- Reflecting on people, events, and things for which we are grateful in life. Most people, when asked if they are grateful, either say they are thankful or express guilt that they are not grateful enough. Neither attitude is accurate or helpful. *None of us* are ever grateful enough, so we should aspire to recall what we are thankful for each day. Gratitude is one of the parents of happiness.
- Reading about positive role models and how they dealt with adversity. For instance, Nelson Mandela telephoned Bill Clinton to share with him how much criticism he was getting since he became president of South Africa. When Clinton asked him if it was from the Afrikaners, he said, no, it was from his own people who were disappointed in him. When Clinton asked him what he told them, Mandela responded by saying: "Yes, and I spent twenty-seven years in jail. They took away the best years of my life. I didn't see my children grow up, it ruined my marriage, and a lot of my friends were killed. And, if I can get over it, you can too! We've got to build a future."

There are many other initial steps we can take to enjoy our life more fully and share it compassionately; the nourishing recommendations just mentioned, and the brief examples to follow in this book, to which you can add your own notes, are but a few. Essentially, we need to be aware of the importance of our own *inner rivers of spiritual clarity and refreshment* because we, too, have a future to build! Be well.

Introduction
Navigating the Road Ahead

As you read this book, I offer three suggestions.

First, after you read each reflection, spend a few moments in silence and solitude to ponder what you wish to take from each entry.

Second, settle on a key word or theme to carry with you throughout the day to see how it psychologically and spiritually blossoms for you. In this way, you will be making the theme yours by letting it come to life given your own history, experience, personality, and spirituality.

Last, and most important, when reflecting on the passages, seek to balance clarity with kindness. When we are only clear about our ways of thinking, perceiving, and understanding our approach to life, we risk being too hard on ourselves—what in psychology is referred to as "narcissistic injury." Hurting ourselves accomplishes nothing. In fact, it can have the opposite result because behavior that we wince at often turns into behavior that we wink at. We can't continue to find clarity by hurting ourselves psychologically. As American humorist and writer Mark Twain once noted, "Kindness is a language the deaf can hear and the blind can see."

Similarly, we can't simply be kind to ourselves because we would never face what needs to be updated, challenged, or changed in the way we approach life. However, when we balance clarity with kindness, we begin to feel a wonderous spiritual awakening that "makes all things new" in our lives. In these dark times, we *especially* need kindness.

THE ART OF KINDNESS

In this way, as you reflect on these passages, allow the themes you encounter to blossom in unique ways—as they only can *within you*—during periods of silence and solitude while wrapped in gratitude for your life.

As the Persian poet, Rumi, is quoted as urging, "There is a voice that doesn't use words. *Listen*." In doing this, you will be psychologically listening, with a sense of real openness, and be able to hear and experience spiritual epiphanies that, at times, speak softly and indirectly—because that is often the way they arrive—quietly and simply.

We Are Not Alone

As the plane from Bangkok, Thailand, to Phnom Penh in Cambodia circled the airport, the children playing on the tarmac hustled away so they wouldn't be hit as we landed. I looked down from where I was sitting and smiled in surprise since it was a scene that I hadn't observed at any other airfield.

Less than an hour later, I was standing inside Tuol Sleng, a high school that had once been a torture chamber used by the Khmer Rouge. I left the classrooms that had in the past formed cells, where you could still see the bloodstains marking the floors, and I stepped out into the sunny courtyard wondering about what I had just seen. I looked up and saw the second-floor terraces meshed with barbed wire so that those who had been interrogated couldn't commit suicide.

I thought, *How are those remaining in this country going to survive this?* My first reaction, I guess, was that this was why I was called here: to see how terrible we could be to fellow human beings. I term it that way because there is no room for projection here. The Khmer people are generally wonderful, so if some of them could treat others in their country that way, we are certainly in the danger of doing the same to our fellow citizens anywhere that we might live.

However, my reaction following this was even more striking, especially given what I had just experienced. It was a deeply felt calling to experience examples of light that were present in the darkness—no matter how profound the horror might be. Over the following days, I would encounter people and events that would bear out this simple but striking experience.

For instance, when I spoke about resilience to a very diverse group of Hindu psychiatrists, sisters of Mother Teresa's, and American Buddhists, among others, who were in Cambodia to help rebuild this country after years of terror and torture, I felt a deep sense of hope given their patience, commitment, and courage. In the process, I remembered the words of the Czech statesman, playwright, and former president, Vaclav Havel, who said: "Hope is an orientation of the spirit, an orientation of the heart…It is not the conviction that something will turn out well, but the conviction that something certainly makes sense, regardless of how it turns out."

I guess a good example of this can be seen in some of the people who are involved in relief work throughout the world. In an interview on public radio, a physician in Somalia commented on our reaction at the time to the starving people there. While people who saw them on TV felt despair, those who met them, those who knew them as more than anonymous faces, had a different experience. Like those who saw the horror of starvation on television, they felt the pain—maybe they even experienced more pain—but they also felt something else, something very significant. It was reflected in one comment the physician made during the interview when he said: "You can't lose hope as long as you are making friends."

This is one of the major lessons I recall whenever I am ever in danger of losing hope in the work that I do in helping and healing professionals and others. This is something I think we all need to remember at times when things seem dark, and we are tempted to pull back and give up. You can't lose hope while you are making friends. We are in this together; we are not alone.

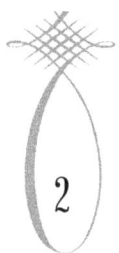

Refreshing Spiritual Rivers

Many years ago, the phone rang, and my wife picked it up and listened for a while. I saw a unique smile appear on her face. She then turned to me and said, "It's for you. It is your youngest granddaughter, Emily. She wants to ask you something."

After I said hello, she quickly said without taking a breath, "Poppop, I am in the third grade now. This is the *last* grade at St. Bernard's School where they host 'special person day.' Can you come and be my *special* person?"

I was touched and could tell it was important to her. However, I feared I had already accepted an invitation to speak somewhere because events are scheduled so far in advance. So, I said, "Well, tell me the date, and I'll check to see if it is open. If I am free, I would *love* to come."

Surprisingly, I had nothing scheduled. And so, I flew out from Maryland to Wisconsin to sit next to her on a little seat in her third-grade classroom to be honored as a special person alongside the other adults who had been chosen by the other students.

As I look back over a number of occasions in my life such as speaking on Capitol Hill, at Harvard, Yale, the U.S. Air Force Academy, and the Mayo Clinic—events that society would certainly deem noteworthy—one of the truly important moments *for me* was sitting next to my youngest granddaughter in class that day. I could feel that I was indeed a *special person* in the eyes of someone I loved, and the honor in being invited by her has remained with me.

THE ART OF KINDNESS

I know that the feeling still remains because, as she was getting ready to leave for classes one year at university, I was tempted to call and ask her, "Do you think you would be willing to forgo going back to college and instead return to elementary school so I could attend special person's day in your class again?"

Of course, I am sure that I would receive a rolling of the eyes as she said, "Oh, Poppop!"

Positive encounters with loved ones form our *spiritual rivers*. They always remain in our lives to quench our psychological thirst for love. In fact, for me, they are also concrete reflections of divine love. In addition, they remind me to relate to others in simple meaningful ways. It truly matters because, some day, it may turn out to be a really important memory for them—one that I am responsible for making when they may have needed it most.

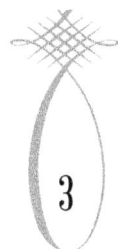

3

Psychology and Faith

Psychology is a gift from God. It is a bit like a "mental shovel" to loosen our inner soil so that a new spiritual tree of life and compassion can be planted. Yet, some misjudge or even fear psychology. And so, they stand with the shovel in hand and look up to the sky and ask God to dig the hole for them. All of us were given the shovel by God. Now we need to use it ourselves rather than asking God to do our job.

Others believe the opposite. They *equate* psychology with spirituality and faith. This is, in a word, arrogant. Psychology is a wonderful gift for us to use, but it is merely a gift to enrich our spirituality. Psychology can never match the depth and breadth of our faith.

In the end, the gift of psychology allows us to see how we are unconsciously moving toward or away from God, and how we can experience and share love more freely and deeply. We discover more quickly when we are merely using religion, religious practice, or sacred scripture not as a way to deepen our faith but as a crutch so that we don't need to face the call to truly love *everyone*.

We also see the need to care for the earth and welcome the stranger as we are called to do. We may upset some churchgoers, but we recognize that following Christ and what he said and did is the true—and only—goal.

Waving the flag of faith but not really practicing it in our hearts and actions is more easily uncovered when we use psychology.

THE ART OF KINDNESS

Domestication of our faith happens less when we have tools to know ourselves and can examine our thinking and fears more clearly.

Hanging a cross on a wall in our room, for example, is done to remind us of the call to walk with God through the darkness, not to demonstrate that we are religious and that our job is done. After all, when family and friends come to visit us, they will not look at our religious signs and believe. Instead, they will look more intently to see if we are living what our mouths and actions proclaim. If our children, friends, and others say, "She is a very religious person" or "He is a faithful churchgoer" and they don't add, "And a really good soul," then the goals achieved by us are not greater actions and aspects of faith but simply religious garb with little substance underneath.

And so, psychology can help us to model what we preach and religiously demonstrate. It is like a helpful shovel so we don't need to use our hands to dig blindly or, worse, pray to God to do the work that *we* should be doing.

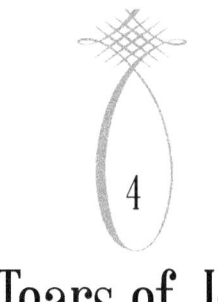

4
Tears of Joy

Several years ago, a young priest and I were driving through a scenic area of New Zealand to a venue where I was to speak. After a brief interlude in our conversation, I asked him a question I often ask physicians, nurses, teachers, clergy, and other helpers and healers who have recently graduated from a professional program of study: "Looking back, is there something that stands out as a 'teachable moment' during your first year out of training?"

Almost immediately, he responded, "Yes. I was in a rural parish and was called to the hospital. However, the young man who took the call and left me a message that I was needed didn't think to write down why, or even who wanted a priest. Since it was a small hospital, I thought I would still go over and find out when I got there."

"As I entered the hospital, I saw a couple sitting in the lobby looking very down. He was crying and she was stone-faced. I went over and asked, 'I don't mean to be intrusive, but did you contact the rectory looking for a priest?' The man couldn't reply but the woman said, 'Yes, Father, we were the ones. You see, we had recently given birth to twins. One was born quite healthy but the other has just died.'"

"After hearing that, we went down to the morgue which was dark. They pulled out the slab with the little figure on it covered with a shroud. We then stood around the body, prayed together, and cried."

"Then, in a resurrection-like experience, we went up the stairs to the neonatal intensive care unit. When we entered, it was a totally different scene. It was bright and cheery! We stood around the incubator and prayed and cried again, but this time, they were tears of joy."

"What was the lesson you learned from this?" I asked.

He paused and answered in a quiet but steady voice, "I don't think it would have been possible for me to cry those tears of joy, if I hadn't first cried those tears of sadness."

Each of us must learn this lesson at some point in life, especially when life is tough for ourselves and for many others.

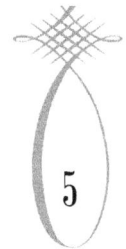

5
The Gift of Prayer

When I sit quietly in the morning, I create a psychological vacuum and, as you likely remember from your high school science courses, nature abhors vacuums. And so, those disturbing thoughts lying just below our normal level of awareness that some call the "preconscious" or "unexamined cognitions" rise to the surface and are given a chance to be aired.

What often rises into my own awareness at such times are my past mistakes, failures, and the criticisms that I have received as a public figure given my books and presentations. Since I am also emotionally thin-skinned, I initially feel overwhelmed. I wonder why I am taking out this time alone in silence, since it opens the door to experiences such as psychological grayness, darkness, and recognition of my failing others as well as myself.

However, a long time ago I received a grace that encourages me to remain in place with a sense of intrigue for what I can learn. The gift was a sense that anything negative said about me—no matter how poor the motivation of the person saying it—is true to some extent, and if I can mine those truths, I can become freer. The same is true about what I might think about myself that is negative. Such information can teach me more about what I subtly and quietly think about myself that is often exaggerated and unfair to me or that I want to run away from rather than face because it may be accurate.

Nevertheless, allowing these thoughts to come and go on their own without either unduly entertaining them or pushing them away is a key element that must be present if I am to feel loved and valued. Maybe that is why when I am alone I also recall the loving faces of those who are close to me and have forgiven me. Maybe that is why I have adopted the Gospel of John and reflect daily on the phrases, "I will not leave you orphaned; I am coming to you.…You are my friend" (John 14:18; 15:15).

Someone once said to a person like me, "You know you have a big personality." On the positive side, that means, in my case, that I love my ability to tell stories and share ideas that may help people as they walk in the darkness so they can gain, regain, and maintain a healthy perspective. On the downside, it means making many, many mistakes, for as Carl Jung aptly noted, "The brighter the light…the deeper the darkness." But then there is love—and God is love—so, in the end, there is much to be learned and embraced. There is a greater chance to laugh at myself when my ego gets too big—which often happens. There is a chance to become freer when I recognize my sinfulness by embracing both honesty and humility together so that my soul can be softened enough to remove regret and welcome new wisdom. I also find that such insight helps me be more reticent to judge others for their failings.

Do you want to take that chance as well? Sit in silence and solitude, and learn from whomever and whatever visits from your past while knowing that you are loved. This is a wonderful way to greet the grace of new wisdom—a psychological and spiritual gift that can finally be unwrapped more completely. At the very least, you will discover that regret is a waste of time (and maybe even a sin) because it chains us to the past, has us think that our sins are greater than God's love, uses up too much of our limited energy, blinds us from seeing the good in others, and prevents us from having the vitality for compassion, including self-compassion. This may be worth reflecting on and bringing to those morning moments of silence and solitude that some of us call *prayer*.

6

Quiet Despair

Most people tend to be very hard on themselves. This is especially (and maybe surprisingly) so for those who have dedicated themselves to a life of compassion. When teachers, physicians, nurses, ministers, and even mental health professionals reflect, they often forget to temper clarity with kindness and humility.

Sitting with different types of caregivers, as I have for most of my professional life, I have found that it is around the tenth session when they share much of their inner darkness. As I listen to their sense of personal failure, professional mistakes, feelings of being misunderstood and not appreciated, I can see and hear the hurt in their lives. I must confess that, even though I have learned the dangers of being overly empathic, sometimes I do go to bed at night with their moments of quiet despair. In addition, they serve as a mirror at times and make me recall my own past sad moments and some of the previous turns in life that I regret because, like them, I have also failed, and failed miserably. (Given my outgoing personality, when I fail…I fail *big time!*)

But, as I reflect about my patients and their sorrows, I think: If only they could see how good they are. If only they could also appreciate the positive difference they have made in so many people's lives. If only they could look back with the understanding that the more they are involved, statistically, the more they are going to fail. If only they could more deeply appreciate that each style of interacting with others is both a gift—and a cross.

THE ART OF KINDNESS

When I reflect on those wishes, I smile and fall asleep knowing that I will not give up being compassionate because I am not perfect. Instead, maybe the knowledge of my own personal and professional past shortcomings will make me even more of an understanding, helpful, and caring person because I also travel in the same dark forest that they do—and still have hope.

A New Life Now

I remember rising early as a little boy on summer mornings to walk down to a small creek in rural New York to go fishing. I never caught anything, but I did get to see the rising sun reflect off the water in such a simple, yet dramatic, way that the memory still comes up for me many years later. During rest of the year, I lived in New York City, where the spiritual awakenings were quite different.

One that stands out was when the pastor of a local parish asked if I would open the church just before midnight on New Year's Eve. He would be away but wanted it available for Lithuanian Americans who were having a party in the church basement. They wanted to come up and pray at midnight to greet the new year.

I got there early to do this for him and patiently waited until they arrived. I had my back to them so when they had finished shuffling in, I assumed they would just say a few prayers. Instead, all of a sudden, the organ sounded, and their deep baritone voices boomed out Eastern European hymns that touched my soul to the core.

Later, after I had locked up and was walking home, I thought: *Why don't we sing like that on Sunday? Why don't I sing like that?* As we celebrate the various seasons of the liturgical year, the call is there for all of us to ask: How can I enter an awake time in my life that is marked by seeing and hearing the message of God more deeply in ritual, scripture, people, nature, pets, and in times of silence and solitude?

THE ART OF KINDNESS

The time is right to begin a new life now. Amid the divisiveness, wars, and disillusionment that mark the world, the time is perfect for a deeper faith. I'll know I am on the road when I am kinder to others and myself and more aware in the now and waste less time worrying about the future. I will know that I am on the road when I am grateful that the spirit of thanksgiving will open my eyes more fully to the people and events that are already in my life. In these tough times, there is a chance for that little boy who once was open enough to experience God in the moment, but had become jaded in so many ways, to return with the maturity of an adult to see even more keenly the presence of the Spirit each day…every day.

A Grace from God

The world craves people who are simply who they are called to be by God. *True ordinariness is tangible holiness.* Yet, being your honest self is difficult if you really don't know who you are. The answer? Spend some time being intrigued with yourself each day. Stop wasting time either being a harsh self-critic or running from your faults. Look for the gifts you have been given and then do three things: enjoy them; share them lovingly with others, expecting nothing in return; and then, see how you psychologically trip over your gifts causing you to behave in ways that aren't helpful. To accomplish this, sit in silence and solitude, wrapped in gratitude for at least two minutes each day. Don't expect that you can hold onto what you have learned. Instead, be like the child whom I once saw in a cartoon: She was coming home from the first day of school and her mother asked her, "Did you learn much at school today?" To which she responded matter-of-factly, "Yes, but they still want me to come back tomorrow." Also, pray honestly and lovingly as a beginner each day, and you will be fine. Trying too hard or not at all doesn't work. Remember that prayer is a grace from God, not a contest, and the fact that you were interested in reading this paragraph means you have already been given this particular divine present.

9
Finding Clarity

Through the centuries, world religions have taught us the importance of having a healthy and clear perspective. Rabbinical scholars remind us that in the Talmud it is written that you do not see things as they are. Instead, you see things as *you* are. In the New Testament, we read, "If your eye is healthy, your whole body will be full of light" (Matt 6:22). In the Upanishads, Hindus refer to turning around in one's seat of consciousness; Buddhists speak of possessing an unobstructed vision.

In support of this, psychologists have also sought to help us to find clarity. They pose such questions as: How are past experiences and views darkening and distorting your present outlook? When was the last time you examined your thoughts and beliefs, especially when you were feeling poorly because of them?

Both religion and psychology focus on how we are mentally painting reality. The reason is that, often when we do so, we forget that *we* have been the artist and see our created images as real and so are unnecessarily experiencing fear and distress.

Running away from our mental depictions of an oncoming train, for example, is exhausting and time-consuming. Consequently, we have little energy to enjoy the gift of life as it unfolds, be compassionate toward others, and escape from the *real* rushing train when we encounter it in life.

A rich, gracious life relies on seeing life as it presents itself. To accomplish this with a sense of intrigue, we must strive to be

Finding Clarity

both courageously clear and gentle with ourselves. Taking a couple of moments each day, sitting in silence and solitude and wrapped in gratitude, is a good way to move toward greater clarity and a healthier perspective. Everyone can spare at least a few moments each day, especially if the quality of our lives and those who turn to us for help and guidance depend on it.

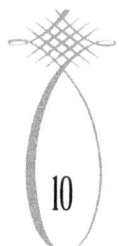

10

The Spirit of Intrigue

A woman who had been abused as a child was finally coming to grips with it as an adult. After a couple of years of therapy, she came in one day, sat down, and immediately began to share something that happened to her the previous week. She said, "I don't know how important this is but the feeling has stayed with me since it happened. I was sitting quietly by myself and reviewing the week as you have encouraged me to do before I come in for each of my sessions. All of a sudden, I realized that I was no longer thinking as much about the past but was more interested in the present. I no longer felt as defined or controlled by what had been done to me early in life, but was more interested in what I could make of my life now. It was like I was being offered a radically different way of viewing things." After a brief pause, she added, "Is this important or am I making too big a deal of it?"

After several seconds of silence to give the moment the respect it deserved, I responded. "To the contrary," I said, "if there would be a mistake, it would be not making enough of this insight. What you have experienced is no less than a miracle." In response, she looked quite surprised, so I then added, "It is a miracle of experiencing love. Love from God and a love by you for your true self that also allows you to have a new perspective toward life that is freeing. It is not that the horrible events in the past didn't happen, but they no longer control or blind you as much because you have experienced the wonderful truths about yourself and they are now allowing you to see life

The Spirit of Intrigue

very differently. The miracle has opened the door for you to envision your own real inner beauty more deeply and aid others to see theirs in ways that most of us, who have not endured the turmoil that you have, can. Yes, it is a real miracle of awareness and compassion that must be honored, for 'you were blind and now you can see.'"

Now, we may not encounter such a miracle as dramatically as she did, however, it is still a grace that we should be open to experience. For instance, when there is an abatement of the negative emotions of hostility, discouragement, anxiety, distress, and self-righteousness caused by a blindness in our distorted ways of thinking, perceiving, and understanding, it is a miracle. At such times, we can see the presence of love and graciousness in our lives more clearly.

And so, we can also have the "psychological mud" over our "spiritual eyes" removed during moments of humility and awareness. We "see all things made new." Will we miss them, or be like this blessed woman who could see the invitation to not let a past she couldn't control upend the present new life that God and good friends were helping her to welcome? We do have a choice, especially when we take out time in silent moments of prayer. Will we fill those moments with a spirit of intrigue regarding God's movement in our lives or merely waste them by judging others, picking on ourselves for our own human failings, or becoming discouraged because life isn't what we demand it to be as a price for our happiness? My hope is that we will choose the spirit of intrigue to enjoy the adventure of life.

The Circle of Grace

When I see the stunning beauty of nature and feel grateful for the experience, I associate the feeling it elicits with a conversation I had with a doctoral psychology student at Hahnemann Medical College many years ago. We were coming to the end of her clinical supervision sessions with me when she paused and surprised me by suddenly asking, "Is there really a secret to a happy life?" I responded, "Well, there are many secrets." "No, no," she said with great energy. "I want you to pick *one*." I had to laugh at her persistence and finally replied, "*Gratefulness* is the one secret."

I then added, "Many people are so concerned that they have been cheated, are not getting enough, want to feel that they got a better deal than others, fear they are being taken advantage of, or are worried that they have contributed too much, that they miss receiving the gifts that true gratefulness brings. Deprivation early in life only makes this pattern worse. When I witness this in people, it makes me sad, especially since a little gratitude would open the door for them to have the eyes to see how much is presently in their lives, including those who have been kind to them. When you do the work I do as a therapist, supervisor, and mentor, you know that gratefulness leads to happiness…not happiness to gratefulness. It is certainly something worth reflecting on or, if you are religious, praying over."

Moreover, grateful people can give with a sense of *mitzvah*, giving and expecting nothing in return. Whereas, people who are

The Circle of Grace

entitled, needy, or have a fear of losing something, miss the chance to be truly compassionate. When this happens, the world, and they, miss out on the circle of grace that is experienced when true sharing with others is experienced by both parties involved. I know that I sometimes give with strings attached which changes the art of giving into a simple trade: "I give to you so you had better return the favor." No, if there is a secret to joy and inner peace, it is real gratefulness—not merely saying, "Oh, I know I should be more grateful" or believing you are already a grateful person, which is not true for any of us in all instances. To meet life with gratefulness requires that we start each day, *every* day, with a sense of appreciation for being alive, for our morning cup of coffee or tea, for our neighbors and family, and for a philosophy of life or faith tradition that speaks less about self-righteousness and rules and more about the love we receive and share with others.

A New Voice

Psychotherapists and spiritual guides listen to those who come to meet with them. They don't just hear people out while waiting for their own opportunity to speak. Wise guides *truly* listen.

Listening involves the guides observing and reflecting nonverbal as well as verbal messages so that people seeking new understanding and inner freedom can observe their own fears, anxieties, and doubts. Listening and questioning their own conclusions also helps them to discover the almost buried hopes, dreams, talents, and strengths that need fresh air.

Slowly but surely, people begin to listen to themselves more intently and accurately as well. When this happens, the other voices from the past that had long obscured theirs become less intrusive, overwhelming, and loud.

Then, amid all this, the clinging to other voices is slowly or abruptly released and a new voice clearly emerges—the person's own voice.

At this point, both the therapist or spiritual sage and the person seeking guidance smile inwardly and think: *How lovely to experience the purity of one's own thoughts and emotions. What a lovely sound they make!*

The guide and the person both reflect: *Isn't it amazing that such a voice hasn't been heard before…or, at least, not heard in a long, long time?*

How good it is for them and others to hear it so clearly now.

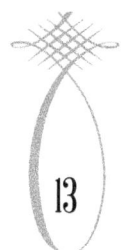

Your Goodness Will Not Be Lost

My morning reflection, especially when life is very active, is important for me. Being centered is essential when delivering presentations on resilience, self-care, and maintaining a healthy perspective to medical and nursing professionals, psychologists, psychiatrists and counselors, social workers, educators, hospital interpreters, chaplains, and other healing professionals.

One morning, the usual happened—the quiet opened to a psychological vacuum in my inner life. Then came a surprise! I recalled a recent episode where I had sent copies of the second edition of my book, *Overcoming Secondary Stress in Medical and Nursing Practice*, to a sister and her religious community in India who were still dealing with the difficult outcomes of the COVID-19 pandemic. When I hadn't heard whether they had received them, I emailed her to see if they had arrived.

In response, she said that mail was sporadic because of the pandemic, and then added, "Your goodness will not be lost."

What a lovely spirit to share—especially when others are feeling down about what they believe they have not done for others, or how they feel they haven't been effective with certain people or situations. I also want to communicate the message I have received again and again:

THE ART OF KINDNESS

Your goodness will not be lost
because your *faithfulness*,
in and of itself,
is a treasure shared.

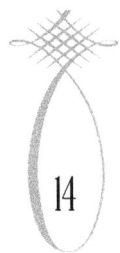

14
Spiritual Mindfulness

Encountering people during young adulthood can enlighten us. During this stage, there is still enough simplicity and honesty left over from adolescence that is now joined with the beginnings of maturity to mark the blessings of life. As one university student said after being asked by her father whether she got used to the gorgeous Florida skies after being in school there for a while: "I know that the beauty of these skies is for everyone here…but I also feel God painted them *just for me*."

Such an attitude is "spiritual mindfulness." Rather than rushing toward our grave and thinking this is practical, we have a choice. Someone once said that "life is something that happens while we are busy doing something else." We are all surrounded by everything that we sense physically. The question is: Will we recognize the gift of such simple things in life? We will if we see them through the eyes of gratitude, take a breath, and enjoy them for a moment or two before moving on.

Moreover, if we are spiritually mindful, we and others in our lives will know it because we will constantly be renewed by the gifts of life we have been given. Because of our unique perspective, we will know they are designated *just for us* each and every day. Not a bad lesson to repeatedly recall during these uncertain and challenging times when we may feel that only something spectacular can change life for the better for us and the world.

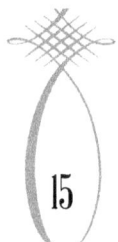

15
The Virtue of Ordinariness

We can sense when we are in the presence of true ordinariness rather than false humility because people who demonstrate it:

- Allow us to fill the room with our life when we meet them because they are content with theirs to let it be
- Have true humility that allows them to honor their gifts while acknowledging their shortcomings with a sense of equanimity
- Enjoy success but know that how one greets failure is the real determinant of greatness
- Don't take themselves too seriously so they don't become brittle, break, and hurt those around them
- Are transparent in a healthy way so we also feel free to do the same when we are with them
- Know that being ordinary, rather than being less, is a sure way to become a small reflection of who is truly extraordinary. This is called *imago Dei*—being made in the image and likeness of God—and becoming so should be enough for us, shouldn't it?

After all, true ordinariness is tangible holiness, and what can be greater than that?

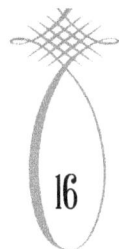

16

Peace versus Boredom

Several years ago, a patient came to see me about the difficulties in her life. She seemed to be most alive during the peaks and valleys. Otherwise, she felt something was wrong or missing in her life and kept looking for either a distraction, problem, or "rush" of some sort.

I pointed out to her that, when nothing dramatic was happening, she should take notice of not only how she felt but what she thought. She asked why I was suggesting this. I responded, "Because I think you have long had a misconception that when your life is quiet, something is wrong or nothing is happening. When in fact, those times are opportunities to relax, renew, be silent, listen, watch, and experience life's nuances, deeper peace, and quiet joy."

What I was really seeking to point out to her was that, since we spend the most time between the peaks and valleys of life, why not explore and relish those times more deeply? This is the perfect time to hear life's quiet spiritual messages so that we can become more grateful, compassionate, and appreciative of the reality of our brief time on this earth. This will allow us to honor more of our moments each day rather than always look to a desire-fulfilled future or remain embroiled in a past we cannot change. Life, *our* life, can really change for the better when we reflect on our quiet, uneventful moments.

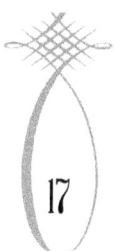

The Presence of Wonder

In uncertain and dark times, we tend to look for something different or for the appearance of unique, spectacular spiritual messages. This is a current and foolish tendency in society because in focusing on the appearance of the amazing, we often miss the messages that are already there and dismiss the presence of wonder in such experiences as:

- A child's laugh
- Chances to help the hungry
- Snow falling
- The smile on an elderly person's face
- Rain softly dropping on the roof
- Kindness from a store clerk
- Beginnings of a new season
- Music from an oboe
- An ocean wave reminding us of unending change
- Forgiveness from those we have hurt
- Seeing the courage in those who are physically suffering, anxious, or depressed.

Oh yes! The messages are there if we can listen or look in new and different directions. And so, our prayer should be:

The Presence of Wonder

Open my eyes
help me to listen
and
soften my soul
so I recognize the "thin places"
where I can sense heaven is with me now
and in my darkest moments.

Waiting for the spectacular to happen only leads to being wrapped in our own ego and missing the wonders that surround us. If something extraordinary does happen, lovely. But by being nourished by what is already there, even if something extraordinary should happen, there will be an even greater readiness for it.

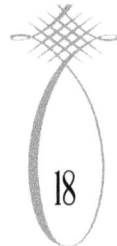

The Birthday Lesson

Spiritual attentiveness is having an eye on the greater lessons God is teaching us each and every day. Paul Tillich referred to this as "ecstatic reasoning," where we are able to connect the immediate with the ultimate. While this is something we should be aware of each day, there is a special time when we are given a lesson for the year—our birthday.

On this day, God comes in a unique way to open us up as we recall the gift of our birth, our individual right to life. It is on our birthday that *the veil is thin* between the tangible and spiritual worlds. Something happens for us to learn a lesson in a deeper, more profound way.

On my seventy-fifth birthday, two fawns showed up just below my deck. After eating their fill, they seemed to turn back and look up, as if to say, "We hope you learned the lesson we were here to teach you," and then left.

What struck me was their *innocence*. It was as if they were being sent to remind me of Nathanael in the grand opening chapter of John's Gospel where Jesus refers to him as a person "in whom there is no deceit!" (John 1:47). This was the birthday message I was given, not simply for myself, but also to encourage others to become more innocent in this age of arrogance, hype, and divisiveness. In other words, I was being called to be more a person without guile who is in a position to purify the spiritual and psychological air for

The Birthday Lesson

myself and others to breathe and make the world a more honest, humble, and compassionate place.

From my deck, I could only quietly utter a few words to the fawns as they left: "Thank you. I'll try." I hope you will do the same.

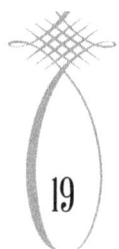

Gratitude, Graciousness, and Intrigue

People come to me asking for…

>Ways to add to their lives…
>>*but* they really need to subtract.

>Techniques to bury or change their memories…
>>*but* they really need to recall and transform them.

>Sometimes people also say that they want…

>More…
>>*but* they will eventually need even more.
>
>Different…
>>*but* this will eventually become the same.
>
>Perfect…
>>*but* there is no such thing or person other than God.

So, what do I say to such people?

I ask them to look in the right direction with gratitude, graciousness, and intrigue rather than with a sense of self-blame or entitlement.

Gratitude, Graciousness, and Intrigue

And, in response, they may ask me, "Oh, so if I do this, I will become a better person?"

To which I respond, "Maybe yes, maybe no, but you will actually enjoy your life more completely and share it with others expecting nothing in return…and that is really why all of us are here."

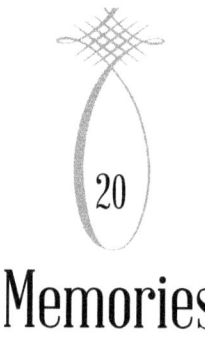

Memories

When it comes to memories, there are a couple of realities that often slip off the radar for most people.

The first is that the only memory that will hurt us is the one that is forgotten because it often sits just below the surface and quietly determines our lives going forward without us being aware of it.

The second concerns whether our memories can be seen clearly and gently so they can take their proper place in our lives. Otherwise, just like the large statue of the cow in most nativity sets, they stand out and make believe they are bigger than the welcoming Spirit of God.

However, something uniquely grace-filled happens when we seek to be truthful and kind and have God walk with us through our garden of memories, even though they sometimes return to our consciousness more than we'd like. We no longer feel naked, vulnerable, and alone.

The memories eventually lose their power, help us to be humble, and encourage us to be grateful. This makes us more gracious in how we treat others and enables us to see God in our lives in surprising ways.

We can never change the past, but we can alter our relationship with it, so that life in the present and moving forward are healing and hopeful. Furthermore, while we will never have wished that negative things in the past to happen, we can be more open to them and deepen as persons in ways that might not have been possible had those events never happened.

Our memories, like the large statue of the cow in the nativity scene, will no longer be a distraction to the One on whom we should be focused. Instead, we can begin to see the past for what it truly was; find the good that was there alongside the hurt, sadness, and loss; and have the small statue of the infant Jesus remind us that, in the end, it is only love that really matters—love of ourselves; love of, and for, others; and the love of a *God* whom we are able to see in ways that truly matter when we are open and humble.

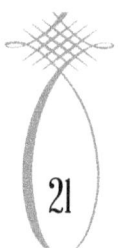

The Evidence of Pure Grace

On several occasions, a patient has come to a session and said to me, "What you said last time really helped." When I ask them what it was that I said that they found helpful, the response is often surprising. It is usually an offhanded comment that I didn't expect to be of consequence.

We are all surrounded by such events in our own lives that we pass off. It is so easy to do. Another person once related a story about encountering an old friend who met her with a broad smile on her face. I said to her, "That must have been nice to receive such a warm welcome." In response she said, "Oh, not really, she smiles at everyone."

After briefly letting her statement hang in the air for a while, I said, "You have deflated this lovely encounter and I wonder why. I don't think if you were vacationing in the Bahamas with a friend and you stepped out onto the beach on a sunny day, you would turn and say to her, 'Oh, let's go back inside because the sun is shining on everyone.'"

Sometimes, this is how we also treat God's love. Because God loves us all, we forget that our particular name is written on the palm of God's hand. Maybe it would help if we slowly read the scriptures more often. In this way, our spirituality doesn't risk becoming too vague. It is also helpful to contemplate the crucifix while trying to be honest with ourselves, "Oh, it doesn't mean much because he died

The Evidence of Pure Grace

for *all of us*." This paradox wakes us up to our attempts to domesticate our faith and the cross, so they lose their power.

Maybe it is time that we also recognize the evidence of pure grace in the small things in life that we do for others and that others have done for us. As the Fourteenth Dalai Lama of Tibet is quoted to have said, "If you think you are too small to make a difference, try sleeping with a mosquito."

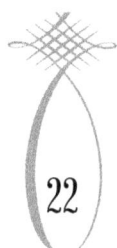

22

Learn to Rest, Not to Quit

I think the humorist Erma Bombeck was onto something when she said, "I think that any man who watches three football games in a row should be declared legally dead."

We often take for granted the need for proper spiritual and psychological nourishment. Instead, we metaphorically eat whatever comes along. This results in simply going through the motions much of the time and "feeding ourselves" with mindless activities and entertainment.

How we nurture ourselves is crucial not for our own well-being but, in the end, for those around us as well. Such nurturing also includes rest.

In the second edition of my psychology book, *Bounce: Living the Resilient Life*, I share my concern about the importance of self-care and provide a "Self-Care Protocol Questionnaire" to help people carefully review what they might do to develop a rich, realistic list of ways to nurture themselves. Even without looking at it, all of us can stop for twenty minutes or so and make our own list. I don't doubt that your life is busy, but if you tell me you don't have the time, I wonder what is more important to you than developing a program of self-renewal. Furthermore, the possibilities for being a vibrant, compassionate presence are so numerous for each of us but for many remain undeveloped because one of the greatest gifts we can share with others is a sense of our own resilience and inner peace, but we can't share what we don't have.

Meditation

A young man once said to me, "I have tried to meditate for twenty minutes each day. It doesn't work. I am distracted for nineteen minutes and only feel I pray for a moment. I am giving it up."

After remaining silent to see if he wanted to add something, I responded: "No, I don't think you only pray for one minute. I feel you pray for twenty minutes and only remember one."

I then added, "Discouragement about prayer often means that you are holding onto your ego and see contemplation as a contest. Let the thoughts come and go like a bird flying by. The thoughts inform you about what is going on in your head. Don't try to bring the bird down or feed it. Let it go. If it continues to fly around, then let it land on the hand of God and say, 'You take care of this. I can't.'

"When this happens, spend the time with a gentle, clear spirit and the grace of God will deepen you. That's much better than simply hanging around for twenty minutes judging yourself about how good your prayer is."

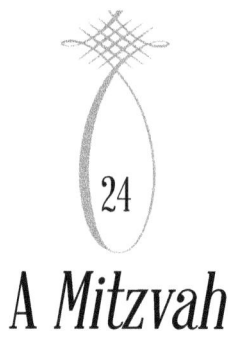

A Mitzvah

When people sit on the rocking chair of worry, they waste a great deal of energy.

When consulting me, they request ways to live better lives. However, if you take on a psychological defense—which is what "worry" really is—directly, you will lose. Worriers tend to be "other focused" in ways that are not helpful to themselves.

Instead, I don't try to help them feel better but remind them that the self is limited. And therefore, the more they worry and are overly involved in themselves, the less energy they have for helping others.

They need to stop being selfish while thinking they are being concerned.

So, the answer is rather simple: do what you can and let others and God take care of the residue.

When they say, however, that they don't see others or God doing anything, I remind them that their job is not ensuring results from others. After all, most of us seem to have trouble in finding ourselves, enjoying the life with which we have been gifted, and sharing it with others while *expecting nothing in return*. It is called a *mitzvah*—a charitable gift that we don't care what people do with or whether or not they are grateful for it.

Doing this allows our psychological and spiritual arms to be free to enjoy and share.

Are We Listening?

When I meet people who feel they have all the answers, I feel pity for them. They are not listening to the larger questions being asked of them in life. Consequently, they remain much less than who they are called to be. It's a good thing that Abram was not like that so he could become Abraham, the father of his people, and Sarai was willing to listen and took the chance of a pregnancy later in life in order to become Sarah, a woman filled with great potential.

Are we listening, or are we like the neighbor who yells the loudest when he knows the least?

26

An Amazing Meeting

Parents have needs, and sometimes they try to live through their children. Some religious groups have many unwritten rules (the hidden ones can really be quite deadly). Society also doles out lessons for acceptance to make the powerful feel secure.

But, despite this, sometimes, in a quiet moment, something marvelous happens.

We get to meet who we *really* are, and the surprise of this makes us truly happy. We are not alone by any means in this experience of pure joy.

Because at that very instant in our heart, we begin to sense the angels and God smiling broadly at us as well.

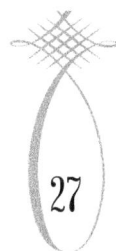

Those Wonderful Scents

The day after I spoke on resilience, self-care, and maintaining a healthy perspective to helpers in Bihar, India, I had the chance to rest at a house in a small village. After waking, I walked out and met a person who had been in the audience the day before. He greeted me warmly and suggested that we take a walk down a small dirt road to join a community of sisters he knew for a cup of tea.

As we walked, he asked me about my family. It was a brief sharing on my part because my wife and I only have one daughter and she was unmarried at the time. I then asked about his family, and he spoke about their colorful life and the many deaths and sicknesses he encountered that resulted in his needing to postpone his entry into a healing profession. Then, almost as suddenly, he stopped, turned to face me directly and said, "But enough of my family. I must thank *you*."

Surprised, I asked, "Thank me? Why?" He responded, also surprised that I would ask, "Why, for your presentations yesterday. You lifted my spirits so wonderfully."

I almost cried. Here he had been through so much and he was thanking me. Then, I realized his gift of *gratitude*. It had changed his perspective on how he saw the world. Because of this gift, he didn't miss or play down anything that was potentially life-giving. I also realized that it is natural—especially if we are caregivers—to forget to be grateful.

THE ART OF KINDNESS

Thich Nhat Hanh once said, "During the war, we were so busy helping the wounded that we sometimes forgot to smell the flowers. Night has a very pleasant smell [here], especially in the country. But we would forget to pay attention to the smell of mint, coriander, thyme, and sage." I was to lecture outside of Hanoi shortly after I heard this, and as I moved up a river in a small canoe, I could smell those wonderful scents. What he had said was true.

May we be mindful and have the sense to do this more often ourselves. This is important because gratitude is the psychological and spiritual soil in which a healthy perspective grows. Yet, we often forget this in a world that is going through such challenging darkness on the one hand and a sense of entitlement on the other. I know I must be more mindful of the spirit of gratitude, which is at the heart of a happy life, but seems to be a well-kept secret today.

28
You Decide!

I still remember being taught not to do "it" by guides through the years, but I find the lesson so easy to forget. I guess that is because, *in the short run*, "it" has so many rewards, and we feel we are saying and doing something that seems right for ourselves.

First, with "it," I get to ventilate my negative emotions.

Second, there's a good chance I can stir up other poor souls with similar issues to support me. We can then form a psychological and spiritual complaining club.

Finally, the result is that I don't need to change my own life, attitude, and style one bit. How great is that?!

There's only *one* problem that I have to deal with when I do "it." So, what's the difficulty in doing "it" now and for the remainder of my life?

Oh, you want to know what "it" is and what the one problem is in continuing to do "it"?

The "it" is blaming other people, groups, and events for my ongoing problems with the world.

The problem with doing this, though, is that in giving away the blame, I also give away the responsibility, need, and *power* to change by listening to prophetic voices and experience a more meaningful and rewarding life.

I guess, in the end, "it" must be OK. After all, so many people do it—especially those who agree with blaming others. After all, if we blame the other gender, persons with a different political or religious outlook, or another race or creed, it's easier than striving to see clearly or think more critically ourselves. If we did this, we would need to pick up our own psychological and spiritual pallets and do something constructive to become a better person.

Essentially, you decide whether you want to be intrigued by uncovering your own role in forming your future or you wish to blame others for your life. No, *you* decide! How you answer will determine the opportunities you are able to unveil and enjoy or whether you wish to rest on your complaints. Your call each day is to do this—and so is mine. (I wish it only applied to you.) And remember, it is the very people like Nelson Mandela, the former president of South Africa, who was locked up for years during apartheid, and others who have truly suffered so much at the hands of injustice who, in the end, *let go* so that they could take their role and initiative in making the lives of others so much better. In Mandela's own words, "As I walked out the gate that would lead to my freedom, I knew if I didn't leave my bitterness and hatred behind, I would still be in prison."

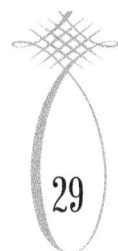

Making Wonderful Ideals a Reality

On two occasions, I flew into Atlanta and drove over an hour to northern Georgia. If I were traveling there simply to enjoy the beautiful scenery and welcoming people that would have been a sufficient reason for making the journey. However, the primary goal of these two trips was to speak to educators with a unique purpose.

They were committed, talented, and compassionate people, who taught in or administered a program that went from 4 p.m. to 9 p.m. It was designed for motivated high school returnees who wanted the opportunity to finish their educations. These young women and men would have been left out of being a part of the future of America if it weren't for these programs—that were led by very special people.

The leaders and educators were often those who had retired from teaching and other key positions in society or were young energetic teachers who were willing to also work with students after their normal hours. By taking a role in this special mission, they clearly demonstrated that they knew what is meant by the saying, often attributed to Aristotle, that "educating the mind without educating the heart is no education at all."

They were committed individuals and the program's overall approach included such elements as individual guidance, assistance in job hunting or connecting with colleges, helping the students see that not only was success possible but—possibly of greater import—that learning how to deal with failure was part of raising the psychological and spiritual bar in life.

We are often taught in the blaring sounds of negative comments from some neighbors, family members, and the mass media, what is currently *wrong* with society, religion, government, education, and other institutions and people we know either personally or through their fame. However, we also need to learn about *the rest of the story* where people and organizations, like the ones I encountered in northern Georgia, are looking to the future by asking the questions: *Who is left out?* and *How can we help with a sense of vision and excellence?*

Finding the answers to these questions can help us see others who are doing the same. We will also recognize that we can join many other good people in becoming the rest of the story that is both hopeful and possible when we act together to make wonderful ideals a reality. Knowing what is *right* in this world is just as important as knowing the challenges we face. Because in doing so, we have a direction and a chance to take the next step in making life better for others and, in the process, ourselves. Isn't this what living a meaningful and rewarding life is about?

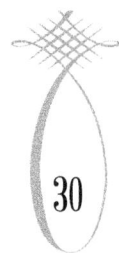

30
New Spiritual Wisdom

As noted earlier in this book, people today are not necessarily physically tired—rest can relieve that. Instead, many of us are psychologically and spiritually exhausted, and this requires something different. It needs an approach that will lead to inner peace and new spiritual wisdom that is actually dependent upon what everyone is going through now.

In psychology, there is an experience that we refer to as "post-traumatic growth" (PTG). This occurs when a person experiences a new sense of meaning making in life and personal depth that *would not have resulted had the trauma or stress not happened in the first place*.

The person, of course, does not seek stress—that would be akin to masochism. There was a time when a misunderstanding of religious principles had some people seeking pain and suffering. The resulted in a form of religious masochism. We don't need dramatic self-inflicted pain. We encounter enough stress in life even when we seek to be compassionate.

In contemporary society, COVID-19 has introduced more people to unavoidable psychological and spiritual exhaustion than ever before. The question it leaves us with is: How can we best face it? While there are many responses to this question, one of the key approaches is to have a realistic sense of the stress we are experiencing on the one hand, and to be open to where it may take us personally and spiritually on the other.

THE ART OF KINDNESS

This attitude will not lessen the pain. However, it will trim the unnecessary suffering and put us in a position to grow personally, deepen spiritually, have a new sense of meaning in life, and, finally, allow us to enjoy the simple gifts of life in ways we may not have before. While we learned to *physically* distance in the past, we can now appreciate more than ever, the great importance of not *socially* distancing from the circle of friends we have who challenge, encourage, tease, and inspire us to be as healthy as possible.

As often noted in my lectures, the French Jesuit priest, scientist, theologian, philosopher, and teacher, Pierre Teilhard de Chardin, once quipped, "It doesn't matter if the water is hot or cold if you have to walk through it anyway." Walk through these tough times we must. However, what we will learn and experience because of this journey is up to us.

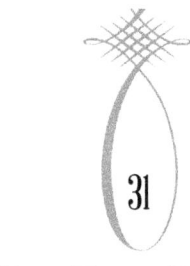

31

The Two Roads

Maintaining a healthy perspective amid the darkness of life often requires taking two roads. The first road is to honor the pain, confusion, helplessness, anxiety, and anger that we feel in life. If we aren't honest about the negative things that happen to us, we run the risk of playing them down or going down the dead-end roads of "spiritual romanticism" or "holy masochism." Either downplaying or inviting the pain we experience for religious reasons is foolish. We experience enough pain at different points in life without adding more.

The second road is to become aware of the suffering of others. This road puts our own pain in perspective and allows us to realize that we are not alone. Others also face terrible things like we have. When we take both these roads at the right time and in the right way, we are then able to model self-respect and honesty about the hurts we experience and appreciate the pain of other people. Following this, and if we can let go of our own situation enough, we will become compassionate toward others in ways that are more sensitive than before. We can recognize more deeply that we are part of one family in God—and that changes us and those who are fortunate enough to meet us.

Finally, by taking both roads, we discover something very wonderful and strong about ourselves. The philosopher, theologian, and mystic Meister Eckhart uncovered at one point in his own meditation that there is "a place in the soul where you have never been wounded." So beautiful and strong.

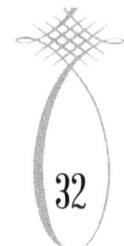

Enjoy the Moment

An older man once shared with me an important insight he had on life. I noticed, however, that although what he indicated was wonderful, his facial expression and voice didn't seem as thrilled they should have. And so, I commented, "Even though you have shared an important awakening in your life, you don't seem very happy about it."

He said, "Oh, if only I had known this earlier in my life."

After a moment of silence, I asked, "How many moments can you be truly alive in each day? The present moment or past ones?"

"Why, only the present one, of course."

"Then why not rejoice in the insightful moment you are in rather than looking back to the past? If you had a wonderful meal in front of you, I feel almost certain that you would enjoy it fully. Moreover, it is the only one you truly have now to taste and relish. Letting it get cold by sitting there lamenting what foods you might have had before would seem wasteful, and I am sure you wouldn't do it.

"It is the same with insights. You can only enjoy the ones you have when you are ready. The past is dead. Let it lie peacefully and be thankful you are now ready to understand something more deeply. There are many who will never be granted this grace, whereas you have been freely offered a beautiful gift. Now that you have finally opened it—*enjoy!*"

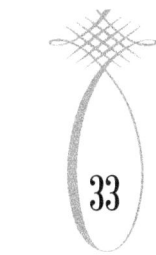

33

Your Quiet History

The day started actively but then the afternoon slowed down and the evening became still—pure, quiet, and still.

Memories started returning but only the small, happy, almost forgotten ones.

I recalled the Friday evening dinners with family, the small talk with in-laws punctuated by laughter and fun.

There were walks on the avenue to visit local stores and share stories and quips with the owners.

Some of the events were larger, too: how I planned and envisioned a new and unique academic program with a friend and worried whether people would enroll in it.

There were books to write and the hope that I would change the world with them—even though sometimes the sales were not great.

What a quiet history I have had to dip into and be truly grateful for this evening.

All of it holds me and reminds me that I am still making a quiet history of my own, but somehow, I am enjoying it earlier now. Soon it will be too late.

When I am asked to guide people, I always inquire either directly or indirectly: What is your quiet history? This is the question I ask you.

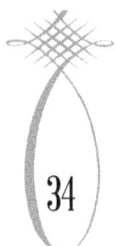

34

A Rich, Compassionate, and Meaningful Life

A friend who knows that I love writing, recently asked me how many books I have written. When I told him, he stopped for a few seconds and said, "Bob, I think you need to get out more often."

He then asked, "Which book should I begin with?" I already had in my mind to suggest the titles that, for some reason, gave me a particular joy to write, such as: *Perspective*, *Night Call*, *The Simple Care of a Hopeful Heart*, *Bounce*, *Everyday Simplicity*, *Prayers for Uncertain Times*, and *Riding the Dragon*.

He surprised me by asking, "What are a couple of quotes you have written that you want to be remembered for because you consider them to be most important for living a rich, compassionate, and meaningful life?" Obviously, I have friends that just cut to the chase.

After reflecting for a moment, I realized that, in both my presentations and writing, there are two statements that reflect the essence of my philosophy, psychology, and spirituality.

The first is: "When you take knowledge and you add humility, you get wisdom. Then, when you take that very wisdom and add it to compassion, you get love. And, love is at the heart of a rewarding life. For those who are religious, God is love."

The second deals with the importance of a healthy perspective

A Rich, Compassionate, and Meaningful Life

in which we don't play down the negative in our lives but are open to how it can enable us to become deeper. It is: "In the end, it isn't how much darkness there is in the world, our country, our family, workplace, or even in ourselves that matters. Ultimately, what is crucial is how we stand in that darkness."

For me, humility, love, and a healthy perspective are worth seeking, strengthening, and sharing. I guess that is why most of my writing centers itself on resilience, self-care, self-knowledge, "unlearning" what is no longer true or helpful, and compassion.

What quotes do you wish to be remembered for?

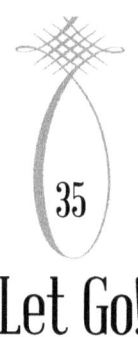

35

Let Go!

When morning breaks, there is a newness about life that is so joyful, freeing. When it happens, not only do I have a feeling of possibility, but I sometimes think of an event that occurred long ago.

I was in training in Quantico, Virginia, to become an officer with the U.S. Marine Corps. As part of this training, we were introduced to the "confidence course" that should really be renamed "the fear and futility course." After being challenged to master several seemingly impossible obstacles, I was surprised to come across what seemed to be a relatively easy challenge. It was an A-frame over a ditch with a rope hanging from it. The goal was to grab the rope, swing over the ditch, and keep going. The drill instructor demonstrated it and it seemed easy. I thought, *Isn't it nice that they want to give us an obstacle like this to build up our confidence before we have to face additional really difficult ones?* (I was quite naïve back then.)

While observing the candidates ahead of me, I noticed that this obstacle wasn't as easy as I had originally assumed. One candidate tried to swing over and swung back. Another swung over and let go after his feet touched the ground and ended up falling back into the ditch.

Finally, it hit me that there was only one way you could do this obstacle. You needed to run up, grab the rope, and *let go* in mid-air. If you waited until your feet touched the ground as a way to feel secure, you would not succeed.

Let Go!

    The obstacle was a metaphor for life. In many instances, if we are unwilling to let go of what we are holding onto for security, we will not be able to move ahead in life. Instead, we will fall back into the ditch of past thinking and beliefs rather than unlearning and being able to be open to new experiences and people as well as different, more unique ways of facing our lives. *Let go!*

36
Faithfulness

When my phone rang early one Sunday morning, a voice that I knew was the head of psychiatry said, "You're going out to the hospital to make rounds today, aren't you?" After saying I thought I had a break this week, he responded by telling me which part of my anatomy I should immediately get there—and it wasn't psychiatric terminology! I put my coffee and the Sunday paper down, got in the car, and hoped it would not be heavy patient load.

As soon as I got on the Lincoln Highway, I noticed a bright orange diamond on the back of a vehicle up ahead. *Oh, no!* It was an Amish buggy that I followed all the way to the entrance of the hospital parking lot.

When I got onto the floor and checked the patient load, I saw I only had two people to see and breathed a sigh of relief, since I had been working seven days a week for some time. The first was a small Amish boy. His buggy had been hit by a car and he was traumatized. When I came into the room, he simply sat propped up in bed and didn't say much. I did most of the talking and ended saying, "I'll stop in to see you again before I leave."

The next case was in intensive care and was more complex. I got so involved in it that when I was done, I walked quickly to my car, having forgotten my promise to the little boy. As I was getting into the car, I remembered the boy and thought that he had probably also forgotten about me saying that I was coming back again.

Faithfulness

However, I know myself well enough that if I didn't return, I would berate myself for the rest of the day…and probably longer!

And so, I returned to the floor and when I came into the room, he looked up and was clearly relieved to see someone he knew since the whole situation was so strange for him. I smiled at him in return and said, "Bet you thought I forgot." In response, he said in English, marked by a Pennsylvania Dutch accent, "Noo. I *knew* you would remember."

Faithfulness is not something to be taken lightly in a world that often promises so much and usually delivers a great deal less. Sometimes a smile rescues a lost soul in trouble, a few words of kindness put people back on track, and a willingness to listen—not simply hearing and waiting for your opportunity to speak—can make all the difference.

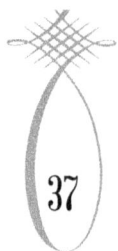

Dealing with Negativity

In my professional career, I have traveled and spoken in several countries at times when those places have been under great stress. Yet, despite the challenges, the people in such countries have always impressed me with their gratitude, resilience, and sense of wonder, and I have always learned a great deal from them. And so, I was surprised recently when I found that I was upset by someone here in America who seemed to have so much and yet always seemed ungrateful and was looking for what he missed or how people took advantage of him. Furthermore, this attitude was reflected in his children, who responded to his neediness and sense of entitlement in their lives.

One was aggressive and always trying to impress him; another acted like an immature adult. The question for me was: Why was I letting his behavior impact mine? I knew it was a unique experience for me because when I asked a friend about it, she simply replied: "Oh, that is the way he is, so why would you let it bother you? He has decided that he is in permanent need, behaves that way, misses so much in the process, and turns people off. I feel sorry for him and for those he has impacted negatively without them really knowing it." It has made me realize that I give away power to people at times and need to know why.

If I can learn about this sensitivity, I can then not only live life more freely but also can have more energy for others who turn to me for help. Knowing what and who affects us negatively, without

Dealing with Negativity

dismissing it because of who they are or how they are behaving, is a great interior journey. I'm in the midst of it now and for some reason it makes me feel young and adventurous. I am also feeling that the energy I surrendered is now returning; just right. (Some advice: The first answer as to why we believe a person is affecting us negatively is usually insufficient or wrong. *Search further!*)

38

Stimulus and Response

Once I was asked to mentor a fellow who was quite jaded and sarcastic. He surprised me on one visit by saying something positive: "I read your book, *Riding the Dragon*, and I really loved it." Happily surprised, I responded, "Well, thank you," to which he then quickly added, "Too bad you're not like what you've written."

After he said that, I began to practice what I preach to new therapists and spiritual guides: "When you are caught off guard by a negative comment, don't immediately react to the stimulus (S); instead, lean back, take a few breaths, and reflect within yourself before you respond (R). If you do this, you will be able to reflect with the person in finding a way forward." And so, in this case, after leaning back and reflecting within myself for a moment, I said to him, "Obviously, by the tone in your voice and what you have just said, you feel that I have let you down in some way. Maybe we can talk about it."

This process of reflecting in the moment before immediately responding is reinforced when we take time in quiet meditation or prayer in the morning as a way to set the stage for the day's interaction. The Buddha was once asked, "What have you gained from meditation?" He responded, "Nothing! However, let me tell you what I have lost: anger, anxiety, depression, insecurity, and fear of old age and death." To this list, I would add the temptation to have knee-jerk reactions to negative comments or actions by others. When I don't succeed in doing this, it is simply a sign that I need to try to remember it next time.

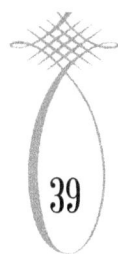

39

The Basic Elements of Friendship

When winter comes, we see the trees empty of leaves, and it is not unusual to feel alone, cold, and sometimes even wonder about who cares for us. At such times, it is good to reflect on several of the following basic elements of friendship that we may have inadvertently set aside.

Have low expectations and high hopes. Often, I have become upset because I have expected too much from people. Even if they are hurting themselves, having expectations of them that they can't fulfill is only providing an added burden to their lives. Even if we mean well, how do unrealistic expectations help them?

Provide limits for people and then let go. Living our own lives according to our own values involves setting limits for people so they don't violate them. Many of us do this because we don't want people to think poorly of us. Yet, let's be honest—people don't get up in the morning thinking of us! And so, set the limits in a relationship and then let go.

Give and expect nothing in return. Many give what they feel is a "gift" of time, money, or a present, and get upset when the person receiving it either doesn't appreciate it or acknowledge receipt of it. Well, a gift is something given without any ties or expectations. And so if you want to give something, do so without any unconscious or unstated expectations and you won't be disappointed.

Don't use yourself as a baseline for what is good for others. People often use their own behavior as a baseline for what is sensible, good, and worthy for others to follow without knowing it. Think of the speed of driving as an example. Have you noticed that anyone who drives slower than you, drives too slowly, but those who drive faster, drive too fast?

Ensure that you have people in your life who have a positive outlook. We need people who can gain, maintain, regain, and share a healthy outlook on life. Determine who those people are and connect more frequently with them, either virtually or in person.

Good friendship relies on time spent in solitude. Although psychology has long emphasized the importance of good interpersonal relations, it is now recognizing that time spent in silence, solitude, and wrapped in gratitude is just as important. One simple way to do this is to take a walk, not a "think." Enjoy the bustling activities of a city or the quiet of the country instead of being wrapped in a cognitive envelope of worries while you are walking. Experiencing your life rather than watching, obsessing over, or avoiding it can be very renewing when you are fully present to it.

40

The Hidden Intentions

One very early morning, I sat alone in silence by the fire, physically tired and maybe discouraged that I didn't or *couldn't* do more for those who were suffering.

As the silence created more inner spiritual space to listen, the usual intentions came to mind: "Lord, be with those who fill the beds of our hospitals, help the poor, and encourage me to donate more. Also, aid those frightened immigrants so they know that they are wanted and loved."

And then I had the unusual urge to pray for people I hadn't prayed for before—in fact, I really had no interest in them and didn't like them. My thought was, *Oh no, not them!* But in prayer we must be open to new callings, so I responded, "God, soften the souls of wealthy TV religious figures who preach success rather than faithfulness and open the eyes of politicians who are truly only interested in themselves and yell hateful divisive words. Please convert men in power (and those who enable them) who abuse women—sometimes even spiritually, using religious words and principles."

Rarely am I puzzled and somewhat sad after a prayer, but I was this time. Then, I realized that in praying for them, I was being called to become even more aware of injustice—not so I would become discouraged or simply blame others, but so I would be even more motivated to do what I could as well as pray for those very persons who were self-serving, fearful, and hateful. It was also a good way to recognize these similar faults, emotions, attitudes, and temptations hiding in my own heart. While we are precious beings before God, we are no bargain at times in how we behave and think.

Strange prayer requests like the one above can really awaken us. I know it surprised me—and possibly softened my soul.

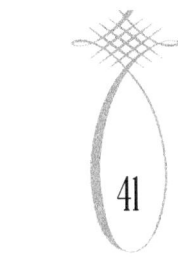

41

Your Own Karma

In my many journeys to various Asian countries, I have spoken on resilience, self-care, and maintaining a healthy perspective when facing great odds. The scenery and food were wonders, but the vibrancy of the people was even more remarkable. They valued family and community and had much to teach me. For me, my visits were a circle of grace. In each instance and in different ways I was called to unlearn and learn anew from the very people I was serving so that I could live more deeply and be more compassionate with others in need. Included in such teachings were the lessons of appreciating the principle of karma—intentions and actions that will have an effect going forward—and the importance of letting go.

It was because of these journeys and lessons that I was primed to learn from a story I encountered in a biography of a true sage. In a biography of a Chinese Zen (Chan) master, now living in the United States, one passage noted the master's plan to bring a large statue of the Buddha along with him on a return visit to China. Upon hearing this, an American friend of his reacted incredulously and asked, "Do you really think the Communist immigration and customs agents are going to let you into China with it?" To this, the Chan master looked surprised and responded: "Bringing this statue into China is my karma. Whether they let me bring the statue in or not is their karma."

In my own life, I have at times felt the call to perform simple acts of unrequested kindness. Occasionally, some people have closed their doors to such acts. When this happened, I had always felt that I was called to persist and then let it rest. Yet, I sometimes responded by feeling blocked or rejected. However, after reading about this Chan master, I felt more deeply than ever before that I should discern what good deeds I am called to share in this life, to do them as best as I can, and then let go. The good deed and actions were my karma, my calling, no matter what the results.

Years ago when I lived in Maryland, I had a gazebo on my property. At Christmastime, I put a small tree in it and would fill it with colored lights and a small star so that those around me could enjoy the season more when they passed by. Some would speed by my house and not even notice it; others who might have seen it from their neighboring houses closed their blinds. But some took notice and told me how much they enjoyed the bright, hopeful message its presence conveyed. They appreciated my positive karma because their karma allowed it; even welcomed it.

How would you have reacted to the sight of my tree? What is your karma?

42

The Faithfulness Business

Years ago, I was speaking in South Africa on resilience and maintaining a healthy perspective to those healing and helping professionals who were trying to rebuild their country after years of terror and torture.

During a break, a woman approached me and said, "I have heard what you said but I just can't do it anymore!" I asked, "What is it that you do?"

"I am a social worker," she replied, "and I help women who have been sexually and physically abused to seek justice in the courts. For this to happen, they must take a day off from work to attend court to present their case. This is difficult because they are poor and are often single parents, but they are determined to get justice, so they go. Then, when I get to court with them, I present their papers to the judge, who is often male, and he frequently says, 'Oh, I haven't had time to read their material…make another appointment!' Don't you see, I am a *total* failure."

She was obviously upset, so I waited a moment to let her emotions settle and then asked, "Who was with this woman, other than you, when this happened?" "Only I was," she responded. "Well, would it be an exaggeration to say that you were closer to her than anyone else in the world at that moment?" "No, it wouldn't," she replied.

And then, I gently asked, "And you want to leave that?"

THE ART OF KINDNESS

After a few seconds, I added, "Don't you realize that, as compassionate souls, we are not in the 'success business'…we are in the *faithfulness* business."

Please remember this when you are reaching out to others—especially during a season of hope like Advent. You are more of a blessing than you realize when you faithfully give with a sense of *mitzvah*—giving and expecting nothing in return. Remember this, especially when you feel discouraged.

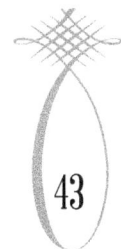

43

Appreciation of Others

This morning, the scene behind my home was stunning. On such occasions, memories come to me with lessons embedded that I need to recall since they are so easy to forget.

In this case, I was reminded of a clinical supervision session at Hahnemann Medical College. I had just presented a case to the supervising psychiatrist. His opening comment was, "You certainly have the psychopathology of the patient down pat, but if that is all you have, you won't get very far and will need to do all the work."

When I asked him to explain further, he said, "First and foremost, as a psychotherapist, you need to see a person's positive traits and help them see them. Otherwise, you will be the only healthy person in the room. When you uncover and share their strengths, they can use them to deal with their current challenges and not just rely on you."

I think this is also important to remember in life when interacting with family, friends, and even those whom we meet in passing. There is so much good in people that we don't want to miss. Moreover, when we are able to mirror their strengths in our interactions with them, they may be able see them more clearly in themselves as well. And this is a wonderful gift, isn't it?

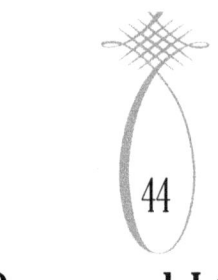

44

Personal Limits

After finishing my doctor of psychology program at Hahnemann Medical College and Hospital, I was gifted with a wonderful, brilliant young psychotherapist to supervise. As we were coming to the end of our time together, I shared with him the following summative statement: "First, what you need to remember is that people have limits that are almost impossible for them to go beyond without true insight. That is why we need to use diagnosis so that we don't burden them with unrealistic expectations—no matter how good they might seem to be at the time.

"Second, they sometimes make trouble for themselves which is often why they come to see us. Try to help them without making them feel badly about their behavior because they have limits. Instead, remember our goal is to help them expand within the limits determined by their genetics and early childhood experiences so that they can maximize their life given their past realities. Occasionally, they may even be able to surpass those limits. But they must do this on their own. We can only set the stage."

Archbishop Desmond Tutu died at the age of ninety. When I think of him and his ministry I realize that he was a person whose concerns for others seemed almost limitless. He wasn't simply interested in himself, his family, race, South Africa, or members of his own faith tradition. He was interested in the welfare of *everyone*.

We will encounter individuals with different limits. Some people's limits enable them to only think of themselves to survive.

Personal Limits

Others only include their ability to be joyous with a partner or in spending time with their families. Still others, like Desmond Tutu, can go way beyond this. They truly flourish by accepting themselves with a sense of joy and peace. They do what they can to understand and share their gifts more fully each day and seek to be compassionate as best they can to all. Is there a right or wrong limit? No. People can only do what they can.

In knowing this, though, there is a special, maybe divine, message for each of us. If we can reach our limit and request that God call us to accept the limits of others, we may be able to move beyond expectations. How wondrous this would be. Such a possibility can come about with the continuous embrace of grace. In this light, when we fail to grow and deepen, as we will, it becomes not a reason to be discouraged but simply a reminder of what the theologian Rudolf Bultmann meant years ago when he said, "Grace can never be possessed but must be received again and again."

So, we need to try to understand ourselves more fully so that we can respond to the call to "act justly, love tenderly, and walk humbly with God" (see Mic 6:8). There is a special blessing in this, no matter how successful we are.

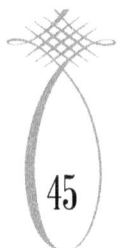

45

The Cost of Presence

More than twenty-five years ago, something happened in a psychotherapy session that I was conducting. It was nothing earth-shattering, but I have never forgotten the message that I took from it; it remains like an old friend sitting next to me on a park bench.

Toward the end of the session, the patient paused for several seconds and then said, "One thing I notice about you. You laugh with me but you never cry." Then she added, "But then I finally realized, yes you do cry…but you do it on your own time."

Psychotherapists, as well as parents, teachers, physicians, nurses, people in ministry, and others who stand with those who seek guidance from them, know enough to practice detachment. Yet, there is still a tangible psychological cost. We must recognize this so that we are not surprised when it happens to us, as I so often am.

Upon returning home from my clinical practice one day, my wife asked, "How are you doing?" Thinking about it, I mumbled, "Terrible." She was surprised because I tend to be an upbeat person, so she asked "Why? Did something bad happen today?" After sitting down in the kitchen without even taking my coat off, I thought about it and realized that nothing awful had recently happened. Instead, I could see that over the past weeks and maybe months, I had absorbed people's pain, as well as their angers, fears, anxieties, doubts, and stresses. The darkness had slowly seeped in. At that moment, I wanted to be anything but a clinical psychologist.

The Cost of Presence

Yet, at times like this, I felt God saying, "Bob, when you say spiritual or healing psychological words, people normally smile or even embrace you, but when things get difficult, you want to run away."

This is true. And, you would think that after all these years, I would remember this danger and be better at expecting to pay an emotional cost for being present to others.

Fortunately, there is one thing that I don't forget, namely, that no matter what happens in my interactions with those who are troubled, I experience real joy and a sense of inner peace as I doze off to sleep at night for remaining compassionate to others.

And so, in place of being impressed by the famous or brilliant, I am emotionally moved by those good people who are quietly being kind in the background, despite the fact that there is an emotional cost for them that even those close to them don't realize.

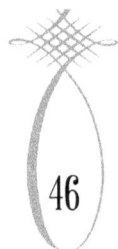

The Beauty of Compassion

Having worked with relief workers who were evacuated from Rwanda during their bloody genocide, being in Cambodia after the Khmer Rouge were pushed north, presenting to caregivers from Aleppo, Syria, in Beirut, and being a therapist for those who were physically and sexually abused, I know the importance of therapeutic distance and the danger of becoming overly empathic. This not only protects the therapist but also allows emotional space for the patients to release their pain without needing to worry about the person who is helping them. Yet, there are times during the quiet moments of the therapist's own life—as in the case of ministers, educators, nurses, physicians, chaplains, social workers, and other caregivers—when a seemingly distant event opens the emotional gates.

Such events may be something like watching a video of LeAnn Rimes performing "The Rose" with the Gay Men's Choir of Los Angeles and hearing her dedication of the song to those who simply want to be themselves and are attacked. It could be listening to a small girl who was successfully treated for cancer sharing her belief that it was also a blessing because it showed her the importance of family. Or it may be recalling the earlier quote from Nelson Mandela like, "As I walked toward my freedom, I knew if I didn't leave my bitterness and hatred behind, I would still be in prison."

In a caregiving role that requires discipline and distance, it is very important to simultaneously honor one's own vulnerability by

The Beauty of Compassion

gently embracing moments of sadness at the pain in the world and within individuals, since it dwells in the same spot as the beauty of compassion. I know I try to do it when I feel the tears during a quiet moment alone. Otherwise, I don't think I could continue to celebrate my work and life, and that would be a shame to permanently lose.

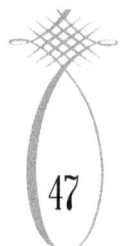

While the World Goes On

A woman has a miscarriage late in her pregnancy.
Wrapped in a blood-soaked blanket
a neighbor takes her to the hospital.

After she physically recovers
she walks out into the street and finds that,
after her absence and loss,
the world goes on.

In another place, a man loses his job,
after many years of faithful work,
stops for coffee before going home to tell his family the
    news.
Yet, despite what has happened to him
others sit around laughing because, for them,
the world goes on.

A nurse confesses that she didn't really know
she had spiritually spent more than she had
until she received a little card of thanks
that made her cry instead of simply smiling,
while the rest of the world goes on.

While the World Goes On

Finally, a woman who watched
her husband die slowly
now needs to find an identity apart,
and after fifty-six years, doesn't know how to start.
And her loneliness expands even more
because amid her sorrow and confusion she sees
outside the funeral parlor door
that the world goes on.

But in all those instances there was one person
who acknowledged the shock, pain, and uncertainty.
Didn't utter platitudes or run from their darkness.
But instead, helped them all recognize upon their
    meeting
that someone could be part of their world for a while.

You see, there are persons who know about pain
and see how a gesture of caring can turn the tide,
so, stop and walk through time with others in need,
while the rest of the world goes on.

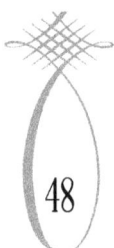

48

Pause before Responding

I was putting the final touches on a presentation to physicians and nurses in the military when I could sense someone standing in the open doorway to my office. I looked up and it was a young colleague looking perplexed. "I hate to interrupt you but do you have a moment?" he asked. "For you, doctor, of course," I replied.

I could see that something was bothering him and that it would take more than a moment but sometimes a disruption is more important than the current project being focused on.

As was his style, he immediately launched into sharing what was on his mind. He said that he was upset about the reactions he was receiving from some of his colleagues and recognized some even avoided him. He was clueless as to what was going on and asked if I would be direct with him as to what was causing him difficulties.

I shared that he was brilliant, articulate, and insightful, but then added that sometimes the very gifts we have can cause us problems. He looked confused and said, "I'm not sure what you mean in my case."

"You seem to be suffering from a 'psychological and spiritual speech disorder,'" I said, "In other words, your unconscious is too close to your mouth. You say whatever comes to your mind without any filter."

While he was absorbing this statement, I added, "In treating patients who have come in for psychotherapy, we are expected to tell people what they need to hear, when they are most apt to be open

Pause before Responding

to it, and in ways that they will most likely receive it. It is not an easy chore with them and, sometimes, it is even harder doing it with ourselves."

I then continued, "Before you say something to your colleagues, I suggest you take a brief pause before responding which is part of the practice of EI (Emotional Intelligence). This will allow you to increase the separation between the stimulus (S)—what they have said to you—and the response (R)—how you react. This will give you a chance to see how you might reply so that it is helpful, kind, and insightful. Your immediate responses sometimes, while accurate, are now also occasionally hurtful, and I am sure that is not your intention—especially when you use humor. Try it, and see what happens."

He did use this approach. Of course, at times, he failed. We all do. However, people began responding to him differently. They could see his efforts at being compassionate and since they valued his remarkable ability to see situations in creative, insightful, often humorous ways, they could benefit more clearly from his reactions.

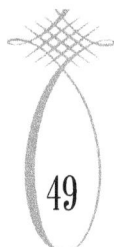

49

Enriching Our Interior Life

Our psychological attitude determines how we live. You can tell if someone has a healthy and rich interior life that gives rise to a wonderful view the world, because it is marked by gratitude, compassion, freedom, and an openness to learn anew.

In spiritual terms, such a life becomes possible when autonomy (our will), theonomy (God's will), and the natural flow of life intersect. The fruits of such a way of being are demonstrated in how we perceive, understand, think, and *act*. For example, some may think that using judgmental "religious words" proclaiming doctrinal principles are permissible, even prophetic. Often, such acts do not reflect true love but rather an unexamined life enabled by a circle of friends who encourage each other but are traveling in a spiritual boat, unfortunately, in the wrong direction.

What might help us turn the boat around or even switch the psychological vessel that represents the current limits of our interior life? The simple answer is humility. When we seek to embrace our gifts, not play them down, and discover our growing edges—defenses and mental blind spots—more completely, we begin to honor this virtue.

Taking time in silence, solitude, and gratitude before God is key. However, this act alone will not suffice, because there is a danger in thinking that we are alone with God when we are really spending time with our own ego. Arrogance, masquerading as principle, demonstrates this.

Enriching Our Interior Life

Having a healthy, holy circle of friends is an aid but also does not suffice. You can even be formed by a humble or brilliant community of confreres and still be worshipping power and lace rather than truly walking with Jesus along the dusty road to Emmaus. The odds against having a rich interior life are indeed great. No one gets a break on this. However, there is a spirit of grace, in which we are invited to start each day in quiet and seek truly good friends who will accompany us, encourage us, make us laugh more readily at ourselves, and inspire us. Additionally, we can read sacred scripture each day for insight and to discover more clearly who we truly are. For, as theologian Karl Barth is said to have once noted: "When we read sacred scripture and ask, 'What is this book saying?' it should ask us in return, 'Who is it that is asking?'"

Reflecting on sacred scripture, life, and ourselves in a spirit of humility and love will help enrich our interior life. We will continue to fall off the road to spiritual wisdom and psychological insight. Nothing can permanently prevent this happening in life. But, with humility and love as our lenses, when we do fall, we will also see God's hand reaching out to help us. We should realize that we need to be open to it rather than insecurely digging in our heels.

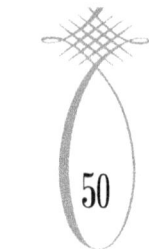

50

The Difficult Book

One day, a colleague stopped me in the hospital hallway and asked if I had a moment. She shared that she was having a problem with a family member. I suggested that she be attuned to the nonverbal language of the person to get to the deeper issue at hand before framing a response.

When she finally took a breath, I said, "You seem surprised that you are having difficulty with this person."

"Well, I am!" she responded. "After all, I am a psychiatrist!"

She said it with such vehemence that we both had to laugh. After all, she was, in fact, a brilliant and quite self-aware physician and psychotherapist.

I then said, "It is obvious that this family member knows your vulnerabilities and how to push your psychological buttons. I think you need to let go of the way you have handled this relationship in the past."

"You mean you want me to drop it?"

"No, simply step aside and let others in the family with whom he relates have more space. If he does open the door again for a relationship, you know as a psychiatrist that you must not enable the person's psychopathology and do it on his terms. He must be open to let go of the belief that people relate in the way he wants when he wants."

She then leaned back and said, "I wish I could remember that the problem is his and not mine and stop feeling guilty about it."

The Difficult Book

"That's understandable. I probably would have the same problem since we care for people for a living and don't readily and humbly remember that our family is like others in many ways. And so, why not take the following simple Asian proverb to heart: 'In the library of every family, there is always a book that is difficult to read.'"

Hold On!

Thomas Merton, an American Trappist monk, writer, theologian, mystic, poet, social activist, and scholar of comparative religion, was walking past a dayroom in his monastery when he noticed an older, fellow monk looking down and dejected. Rather than passing by, he walked over to him and asked if he was all right. The monk shared that he felt down.

In response, Merton said, "Brother, courage comes and goes. Hold on for the next supply."

I think that says it all.

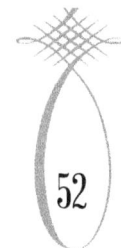

Actively Loving Oneself and Others

Recently, I had the opportunity to give a virtual presentation to spiritual directors in Australia. On a couple of occasions in the past, I had flown there to present in Sydney, Melbourne, and Brisbane, so it was a joy to connect with Australians again, albeit virtually.

To set the stage on this occasion, I outlined and reinforced two key points that they already knew. First, that being a compassionate presence positively impacts others in ways we may never realize. As the Chinese proverb states: "When the tide rises, the boats in the water do as well."

Second, I reminded them of something we often forget in ministry, medicine, nursing, teaching, social work, and mental health as we help others in need: being compassionate and hopeful also benefits *us*. As the physician and humanitarian Albert Schweitzer is often claimed to have said: "I don't know what your destiny will be, but one thing I do know, the only ones among you who will be really happy are those who have sought and found how to serve."

Central to my presentation, however, was to focus on what I felt was the core of what they were trying to model and help others to live out—namely, that actively loving ourselves and everyone is the most important of God's calls to us. Essentially, I noted that their ministry was so precious because they were calling people to integrate autonomy (their will) with theonomy (God's will), so as to become freer within, and to *act* in loving ways with others—including those they may never meet.

As helpers and healers, they and those they were guiding (and all of us) were being commanded to become more aware of, and respond to, the challenging question that the Benedictine Godfrey Diekmann once posed to Christians: "What difference does it make if bread and wine turn into the Body and Blood of Christ if we don't?"

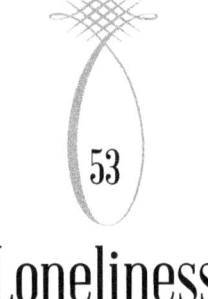

Loneliness

One of the least understood and under-honored challenges in life is loneliness.

Part of the reason for this is that it often makes us very uncomfortable whenever people express it. After all, how can we respond to such a difficult, unanswerable, existential question? Furthermore, it keys into our own sense of being apart. It is really tough!

When therapists, mentors, and spiritual guides have asked me about it, I am truly grateful that they trust me with such a sensitive and personal issue.

In return, I admit to my own loneliness, my periods of feeling separate and not truly understood, accepted, or appreciated. I share with them that, even if many people know about you, it doesn't mean that they feel close to you…or you to them.

You sense that they felt understood—not simply as helpers but as human beings. You can see the smiles on their faces and their bodies relax.

Even those who feel loved can still feel that vague sense of emptiness. Maybe they have lost a loved one and, even though they know they were fortunate to have such a great person in their lives at some point, the quiet gray pain remains that no one truly seems to understand. After all, they probably can't either.

Others are surrounded by friends and family who are in a word, "terrific." Yet, while being surrounded by and being grateful

THE ART OF KINDNESS

for this, in the quiet of a night or on a rainy day—or worse, a sunny day—they feel alone.

As I sit with people who are experiencing this sense of loneliness, I don't try to make them feel better. That would be disrespectful to their poignant sense of loneliness. Instead, I sit with them in their helplessness and don't try to run. When the timing is right, I let them know that they deserve to appreciate that while nothing can take away the pit of loneliness, because they are good souls, they deserve better, so maybe we can look together for the love that is already in their lives as a sign that the love they want can still be reflected in some way, in some people, in the now.

When they leave, and since I find great understanding and solace in scripture, I recall the words in John's Gospel: "I will not leave you orphaned; I am coming to you" (14:18) and "You are my friends" (15:14). I close my own eyes in prayer, knowing love is there for me to share with others who are having a tough time, but I also need to know, in the end, the only cure for loneliness is God. It may be reflected in loving people around us, the beauty of a summer's morning, or the wind blowing through the trees but, in the end, it is still…it is really…*God*.

54

Caring for the Caregiver

The public often makes two errors about those who interact with people who have suffered great pain and trauma early in life. It is based on a failure to realize that there are three basic types or groups of response to trauma in life and that trauma has far-reaching effects beyond the person who has been horribly and unforgettably treated by others—often by those whom they trusted.

The first type of response concerns those who totally amaze us. They are victims of extreme and brutal stress and trauma early or later in life and do not play down what they have been through but allow those fires of suffering to soften their souls so they can see life in new, meaningful ways that those of us who haven't been through such spiritual scorching cannot. Psychology refers to this as new meaning-making and post-traumatic growth; in religion it is regarded as the wisdom and depth that results from the spirituality of suffering.

The second group responds to undeserved pain undergone early in life in a way that they must use all their energy to stay afloat. Therapists and spiritual guides see this challenge and try to help them as best they can.

The third type is the toughest for helpers and healers, family, and friends to assist. This group of people spend the rest of their lives feeling entitled so that those around them must continue to pay and repay for the suffering they experienced early in life. The sadness is that, in doing this—something that I am not sure they can really help, since it is an unconscious movement of which they are not aware—is that their family and friends are drained by their ongoing need to be supported and encouraged. And so, their lives are distorted by the need to support their father, mother, sibling, friend, or significant other.

I have seen it in the children of survivors of the Holocaust whom I treated and in those who had difficult times early in life, and then in their spouses and children, who are "only trying to help," while the trauma victim was the one who really needed to support *them* but couldn't…and didn't.

Since I have had to deal with this final category of response to early trauma, I can well understand that this is *truly the best way that they can respond*. The reality, however, is that if I drop a rock on your head either by mistake or on purpose, you still get a bump. I have often felt sadness both spiritually and psychologically when I realize the pain that has resulted from a long-ago trauma that the trauma victim continues to endure and has then resulted in a passive, quiet pain that others have had to bear for them.

If you are one of the people impacted by another's trauma—family, friend, therapist—please know this so you don't lose your way because of a horrible injustice that happened long ago to someone you love. Just as the trauma victim needs love and support, so do you!

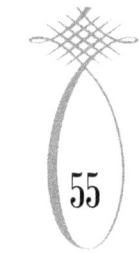

The "Cana Effect"

Without any planning, in both my work and life, I have interacted with many brilliant, creative, dedicated, famous, (and infamous) people. This has been a double-edged sword for an unusual reason: these people were and are so very talented.

Recently, for instance, I came across a person who is both passionate and compassionate and who is sensitive, knowledgeable, dedicated, and accomplished. In our discussion, however, I could sense by his nonverbal communication and how he was questioning me about some of the feedback I had given him, that he had already made up his mind even before he walked into the room.

In fact, I had to stop myself from laughing when he used some of his wonderful talents to avoid, "creatively" reframe, and resist looking at the issues about which he had come to speak with me. Gosh, he was good at being defensive! I was clinically impressed. His stated wish was to face life in a new way given the different phase he was just beginning to enter, but his behavior was very much to the contrary.

It was admirable the great motivation he had for living wonderfully, but like many of us, he was turning a corner and couldn't see as clearly as he had in the past. At some level, he was afraid of appearing foolish, as we all often feel when change confronts us.

Although I don't have his fine talents, I find that I sometimes do the same thing. I don't see the new phase I am entering as thrilling, enlightening, and *necessary*. Instead, I stay comfortable with what I am doing and mistake this comfort for peace and being true to myself.

THE ART OF KINDNESS

When I am fortunate to recognize what is happening, I always go to the top and think of Jesus. In this case, it is when I imagine him being relaxed and enjoying himself at Cana, when who should appear but his mother! She wanted him to do something (change water into wine)—a miracle that would launch him into the next phase of his life, his public ministry. While many are moved by the miracle he performed—how could you not be?—I am more deeply touched by what I call the "Cana effect." At Cana, he receives the message from his heavenly Father, through his earthly mother, what he must do to move into the next phase of his life and ministry. Initially, he resists, but the story doesn't end there for Jesus nor for us.

How often have I resisted epiphanies in my life because the source didn't seem "right" or I felt the timing was off? How often have I dismissed what someone has said to me because they lacked authority or impressive credentials? And so, I have missed their messages that would significantly change my ministry and life for the better. They were being faithful to what was being asked of them, but I wasn't.

Would I respond to requests to see life in new ways with the dismissive words, *Oh, that is just how I am. It is my style. That is how I was raised. It is because of what I went through early in life?*

It is important that we all honor the Cana effect. We need to keep our eyes and ears open to what emotions are stirred within us—even if they are negative. In fact, they may be signaling something that is needed so much more as we move ahead in life.

We do have a choice, but God may want us on a road that we haven't traveled before because the timing is *now* right for us. Moreover, this is not just about us but about others, who count on us to grow and be open. For Christians, this may be the call of discipleship. We do have the choice to remain comfortable in remaining the way we are, and feeling justified in doing so, or we can take the road less traveled by us—the one God wants us to take and that detours from the past. We must remember that the good news is often not resisted because it is good but because it is *new*.

56

Feeling Lost

Often when people come to me and say that they feel lost in this world, it turns out to be a good sign even though it may not be pleasant at the time. Instead, it is a call to move away from asking the question, "Where am I going?" so it can be gratefully replaced with an interest in responding to, "With whom and where am I *now*?"

Such a question brings us prayerfully and mindfully home. Consequently, we can experience our lives more completely, rather than spending most of our days in a cognitive cocoon wishing or worrying about tomorrow. The real spiritual food before us is far more satisfying than wasting time consuming a mental menu that only makes the warm gifts already present in our lives become cold.

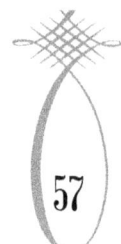

Lifting the Heavy Bales

Occasionally, something happens and I don't realize its impact on me until a memory comes forth and I reflect to see what prompted it.

Such was the case when I woke up one morning and remembered an interaction with one of my uncles on his farm. I was standing alongside him and commented that the workers in the field didn't seem to be lining up the bales of hay in the wagon properly. He rarely said much to me so was surprised when he looked over at me and said, "Don't be like the fellow sitting in the buckboard by the road, drinking beer, and correcting the workers in the field who are doing all the haying."

People often claim they have a right to their opinion, but they also have a responsibility to educate themselves and respect those who are in the field lifting the heavy bales.

58

Tears of Renewed Wisdom

An Orthodox priest sent me a note from the mayor of the city of Mariupol, Ukraine. He wrote,

> *Six-year-old Tania was pulled out from under the rubble of a destroyed house. We cannot say how long our little strong Mariupol girl was fighting for her life. We cannot even imagine how much this innocent child suffered. She was alone in the last minutes of her life, exhausted, scared, experiencing terrible thirst. This is just one out of many stories of the city of Mariupol, Ukraine, that has been undergoing a Russian occupation blockade for 8 days in a row.*

For the past forty years, my work has been with professional helpers and healers on the prevention of secondary stress—the pressures experienced in reaching out to others. These efforts have taken me to the Mayo Clinic, the Yale School of Nursing, and to twenty countries where people are living in stressful situations. And so, I have seen a great deal and written much on self-care and maintaining a healthy perspective within the darkness, and in the spirit of post-traumatic growth, even how people grow *because* of the darkness.

And so, when I received the above message and read this story of a little girl named Tania dying in the cold, alone, frightened, suffering, and dehydrated, I had heard similar stories before. Yet, this time I cried and felt overwhelmed. This surprised and concerned me because I knew that, if I felt helpless and hopeless, I would be of little use to other professionals in need. This was not just about me. What could I do so that, in some small way, the experience of this small, lonely, frightened girl who died without her mother, father, or a friend present to even hold her hand, would not be in vain?

I reminded myself that I didn't have the luxury to sit on the sideline and do nothing. While I couldn't prevent Tania's awful death, I could do something to honor her. The following ideas came to mind.

Remember. I would not forget or let others bury the horrors of war that are lived out in the lives of innocent people while government leaders who perpetrate war, hunger, and abuse—often in the name of nationalism—sit in safety. The response that "I didn't know what was happening" wasn't an excuse during the Holocaust, and it isn't an excuse now.

Let my upset be the fuse for action; not helplessness. If I simply became upset and felt overwhelmed, nothing good would come of knowing about the carnage. Instead, determining what actions I could take such as donating money, raising people's awareness, and encouraging others to become involved is an initial response that can open a door to learning what new steps can be taken.

Give birth to a healthier perspective. Although I must honor the pain in my own life, knowing about the dire suffering of others should help me put my own situation in perspective. This will help me avoid magnifying my own inconveniences and problems as well as becoming too self-involved. Such horrors should also help me embrace more fully the heart of happiness—being truly grateful for all I have.

Initiate new meaning-making. Sad events in one's life can deflate us, or they can lead to asking ourselves what is important in life. With new experiences comes the opportunity for new selflessness and humility.

Tears of Renewed Wisdom

    Essentially, it is not the amount of darkness in the world or ourselves that ultimately matters. It is how we stand in that darkness that is crucial—a healthy perspective makes all the difference. I will not let that little lonely Ukrainian girl die in vain. Instead, her death will be the fuse for me to seek to live with more love. In her honor, I will examine again what I can do rather than go down the dead end of feeling sorry for myself because the world is such a dark place. My tears have dried for now, but the terrible stories will continue in this war and life. I must continually search for new ways to be the light rather than surrender to the darkness. There is no alternative. Tania is counting on me and I won't fail her.

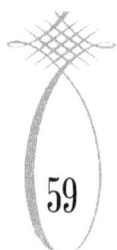

59

A Difference Is Possible

In the Northern Hemisphere, late winter brings cool, damp weather. It reminds us that we are still not in spring but have occasional high temperatures that let us know a new season is almost present. The same can be said about our inner lives. Early springtime is an opportunity for renewed spiritual awakening for all people. In Christianity, this season is called Lent.

During this time, elements of a social and psychological winter remain. Horrible wars, pandemics, as well as societal, national, family, occupational, and personal problems are clearly present. However, in this season there is also a chance for a difference for those who are willing to focus more on approaches that open the door and to a change in outlook.

In the book *One Minute Wisdom*, Anthony de Mello writes that the sage, when asked by the disciple how the spiritual approaches he offers will help him, responded, "As little as you can do to make the sun rise in the morning." The disciple then asked, "Well, of what use are such approaches then?" To which the sage responded, "You will be awake when the sun finally does rise."

In the days of late winter/early spring, we have a choice: we can spiritually remain asleep, or we can become more awake to possibility, hope, and a new appreciation of life. All of us experience darkness in life...*all of us*. Some will become sad until it turns into self-pity; others of us will seek to do what we can, and look for friendship that is challenging, supportive, inspirational, and will make us

A Difference Is Possible

laugh at ourselves when we take ourselves too seriously. We will also seek to develop a rule of prayer like the ammas (desert mothers) and abbas (desert fathers) of the fourth- and fifth-century desert so our lives will not be captured by *chronos* (e.g., values in secular time) but instead be steeped in *kairos* (e.g., values in spiritual time).

The results will be clear for those who take that route, and do it with the help of others, and the grace of God. In response, they will:

- Hear of the horrors of war, poverty, and injustice, *but* they won't remain sad and helpless. Instead they will find what they can do, do it, and let both others and God take care of the residue.
- Experience the disruptions of a pandemic or other undesired changes, *but* they will not jump into the golden casket of nostalgia. Instead, they will recognize that these situations offer an opportunity to see what is really important in life and take these new situations as a psychological stage for renewed creative spiritual meaning-making in life. They will learn anew what is truly important and of value.
- Undergo deprivations in life, *but* such absences will also spur greater gratitude for the simple gifts that are often overlooked—a cup of tea or coffee, while smiling and looking out the window or reading, sitting in a soft, comfortable chair will now be appreciated as pure gift.
- Have distractions in prayer during their periods of silence and solitude while wrapped in gratitude before God, *but* instead of seeing such interruptions as a reason to stop praying, they will fathom that what they teach us what are often undisputed lies roaming around in their heads all the time. When this happens, such unexamined, often negative cognitions—ways of

thinking, perceiving, and understanding—can be disputed and placed in God's hands for healing before returning their hearts to quiet prayer.

Yes, during times of renewed spiritual reflection such as when spring dawns and Lent occurs, for some of us, a difference is possible. Many will walk past the narrow gate that leads to a new perspective. Others won't. Which group will we choose to join? To walk by the opening to a new life is easier. Yet, to stop and reflect on how we can offer *almsgiving* to others, *fast* from selfish, unhelpful behavior, and appreciate the spaces already in our schedule to *pray* more deeply, is to choose the path to a deeper life rather than continue to drift with it.

Failure will happen as those who seek to travel, but continually fall off, the path they are called to. That's not a problem, since it is a reminder that we can't do it alone. We need encouraging role models and God's grace to bring us back on the spiritual road and to help us experience the key virtue of the desert: humility. What a wonderful difference such times of the year make…*if* we let them.

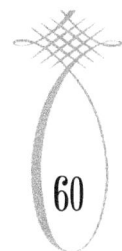

60

Stumbling on God's Love

I was in a coffee shop after a long day and an overworked waitress took an extra moment to smile and be kind—and *I knew that I had stumbled on God's love.*

As I sat in the car driving home after a challenging day working with people who had been traumatized and had a terrible morale, I recalled the words from John's Gospel, "I will not leave you orphaned; I am coming to you" (14:18). In that instant, *I knew that I had stumbled on God's love.*

As the situation got more dire for children in a war zone, young teenagers took the time to see how they could help and, once more in seeing their caring faces, *I knew that I had stumbled on God's love.*

On one Veterans Day, I walked into a store with my U.S. Marine Corps cap, and the manager stopped her work and spoke to me rapidly in spurts: "You were a Marine? So is my son now. We give out cake to those who served on this special day of remembrance," and she rushed to bundle some up for me. As I left the shop, I could feel tears on my cheeks. *I knew that I had stumbled on God's love.*

There are more times when this has happened to me, but I won't bore you with them now. Just let me add: Stay awake! Don't predict how it will happen, and you will also stumble on God's love again…and again. I *promise!*

61
See the Gifts

Someone once shared with me her sadness at rejection, and I told her to rejoice in the gift of the caring nature that she has. Another was exhausted with emotion over injustices in the world, so I reminded him of his pure gift of compassion. Then another shared that people take advantage of her, and I complimented her on her welcome gentleness, but also reminded that she didn't have to immolate herself to warm others. Finally, another individual was upset at negative reactions to her strong comments, and I commended her for her passion and told her that we have enough shy souls already.

To each of them, I made the following recommendations:

> When you are criticized or hard on yourself, turn the problem around to see the gifts that you have; and
> Consider the situations that give rise to you distorting the natural talents you have been given by God.

In this way, you can learn to psychologically *prune*, rather than bury or reject, your spiritual gifts. When we do this, as Jesus taught us, these charisms will not simply be a source of sorrow, self-doubt, or resentment, but with friendship and reflective prayer, they will blossom even more deeply—and how wonderful is that?

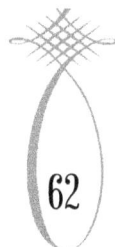

The Gift of Spiritual Sadness

Sometimes, when sitting at a meeting or a family or neighborhood gathering, some people share with me that they look around and see all the faces and sense that they are truly good people, but that they suddenly feel lonely because they feel different.

At such times—and it can even happen when people are by themselves thinking of family and friends—the immediate temptation is to flee mentally. After all, who wants to feel lonely?

Such sadness can become spiritual when, rather than trying to escape it, we sit with the feelings knowing that we are loved by God for the very reasons we feel lonely—we are unique. Our specific names are written on God's hand.

During such times of alienation, it is helpful to recall the many times and different ways that we were loved, accepted, and valued by God:

- The smiles on certain people's faces when we met them—even those whom we may have encountered only briefly
- Both small and major sacrifices others have made for us
- The times when we have enjoyed a laugh with a friend
- Efforts of helpers and healers who inspired us when they aided suffering souls who were undergoing terrible ordeals

- The dogs who may have lived with us for a while…or the cats that let us live with them!
- The food on our tables and the other needs we have had, and continue to have, met
- The beauty of nature in a forest, by the sea, or standing on the edge of a canyon
- The experiences of our own uniqueness in ways that don't simply make us feel "different" in a bad way, but aware of the wonderful signature traits and virtues God has given us to enjoy, develop, and share—in ways that only we can!

So, sudden fleeting feelings of sadness at being separate from others may initially be an unpleasant experience. However, they can also wake us up and tell us to stop and to experience *imago Dei* (the image of God) more deeply. This is a great gift to receive, especially when we are running through life, going from one necessary task to another without being reflective, mindful, or *prayerful*.

The Dalai Lama warns that everyone will die in the middle of a project of some sort. Of course, tasks must be done in life. But just as spiritual darkness is designed to wake us up to how our prayer lives and relationship to God are ready for a change, spiritual sadness is also a wake-up call to stop, take a breath, and live. Someone once remarked that life is something that happens while we are busy doing something else. Experiencing being apart can help us to avoid this tendency, though, by helping us to see anew that, while we are active, we can also be more present to the moment—who we are, and who we are being asked to be for others in a meaningful way. When this happens, the stage is set for sadness to move to gratefulness, new wisdom, self-acceptance, and seeing friendship and community in a more powerful, diverse way.

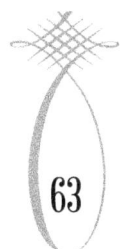

A Loved, Imperfect Disciple

If our difficult memories aren't instructive, don't soften our souls, and make us kinder to ourselves and others who need our gentle presence, what good are they? If they only result in us becoming sad over our past behavior or defensive as to how we acted and reacted toward others, what good are they? It would be better if we were spiritual amnesiacs.

In such cases, just as in the instance of actual amnesia, we need to visualize people from our past who loved us. In doing this, we can then slowly remember our "family of love" and vividly recall Jesus lovingly telling his disciples, "I have called you friends" (John 15:14).

In doing this, we can then see the core wonderful truths about ourselves so that our remaining days include gratitude for the gifts we have been given and can freely share with others. We recognize that we already have enough, simply because we are loved. When this happens, our memories will not be a source of hurt or need for defense, but rather a teacher who reminds us that we are forever a loved imperfect disciple and not God.

Defending the Defenseless

Being in the public eye can be fun and gratifying. The energy of people listening to you, reading your material, and offering stimulating and enchanting responses to what you are sharing is encouraging and a reminder that there are grateful people in this world.

When you stick your head over the wall, you must also expect some to throw rocks. By this I don't mean helpful criticism. Instead it is often someone whose life is upset by the help you can offer them and rather than show gratitude or reflect on what you have said, they become fearful. The bright light scares them because it offers hope. Sarcasm and negative responses are always easier for some than a smile and a word of thanks.

I remember this happening when I posted something online. The responses included, "Are you trying to push your books?" and "This type of post doesn't fit the goals of this site. We just want information that is helpful in finding companies that sell what we want or fix what we have broken." The sad part—and I must admit the most hurtful—is to see other people giving a thumbs-up to such negative reactions.

But then, something comes into your life to remind you that doing what you can to protect others and offer daily hope is worth all the criticism and demeaning comments.

Recently, one of my Facebook friends posted a photo of a sheepdog, covered in blood, being comforted by one of the sheep after having defended the flock from wolves. I was encouraged and

Defending the Defenseless

moved not only by the courage and commitment of the sheepdog but also by the kindness of one of the sheep who had pressed its nose on the nose of the bleeding dog.

As I sat in my own sense of sadness at how negative people can be, I was reminded that such sad events are part of the journey of defending the defenseless and thinking a bit less of yourself. In seeing this photo, a faithful animal had taught me how to be human in the best sense of the word. It also reminded me of the parable of the good shepherd which was Jesus's way of saying that *you need to do this, you can do this, and I will love you for doing this*.

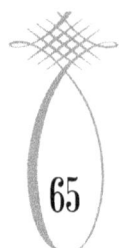

Your Special Day

Birthdays are significant because we and others make them so. It is important to remember on those special days that:

- When you look back at your joys, cherish them as being as real now as they were then.
- If you reflect on your mistakes that you wish you could change, realize that you did the best you could with what you knew and the support you had at that time.
- On the day of a special birthday, enjoy it to the fullest. God would want you to rejoice in the gift of this day and your life.
- Finally, as you look forward, do it with self-compassion, care for others who cross your path, and a commitment to show gratitude to God by enjoying the life that lies ahead.

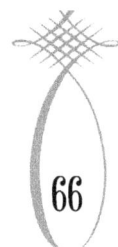

Resignation and Acceptance

Resignation and acceptance look alike but are radically different. Resignation has us mindlessly become unnecessarily comfortable with what is painful or disagreeable to us. Whereas acceptance results only after careful discernment of what we can or cannot change. We shouldn't waste energy on what we can't control; instead, we should wisely face and change what we can.

    Life improves incredibly when we know this difference. Many of us become too *comfortable with the uncomfortable* in our lives when this is neither necessary nor desirable. Devote some time to discernment so that this doesn't happen. Quite simply: I want life to be more enjoyable for you but I need your help.

Our Soft Spots

Recently I pointed out the generous acts of some people in our community to a neighbor. His dismissive response was jaded. The surprise for me was my sad reaction to his response.

I try not to become thrown off by the negative attitudes of other people. Not only do I not want to be impacted by their darkness, I also want my psychological arms to be free to embrace the suffering of those who come to me. I don't want to waste my energy on those who have a personality marked by narcissism, envy, sarcasm, and other defenses.

In this instance, my surprise was that, despite my work in debriefing relief workers evacuated from Rwanda during their genocide and presenting to those who care for the wounded at Walter Reed National Military Medical Center and the National Naval Medical Center, I was still vulnerable to the negativity of this person.

In my morning reflection, my response to this experience was twofold. First, I recognized anew that I continue to have psychological and spiritual soft spots that can use energy that others in true need might require; and second, I recognized the need to take heart from the persons who are doing good in the world in helping out in places such as Ukraine or the local assisted-living center to reinforce my faith in the goodness of humanity.

The question I ask is: What are your *soft spots* and how can you prevent giving away unnecessary joy and peace that you can experience and share with others?

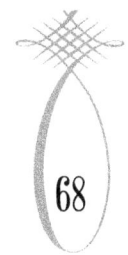

68

A Painful Journey

At my presentations, I am often asked to conclude with a summary of my lessons on resilience and post-traumatic growth/spirituality of suffering. This isn't easy or really possible, but they want something to reflect on and pray over as they continue to reach out to serve people in such settings as Syria, Haiti, and Cambodia. So, I tell them to:

- Honor the real pain in your own life. Not to do so is simply an exercise in spiritual romanticism and of no help.
- Remember the suffering of others in your family, community, country, and the world. It will help put your own plight into perspective.
- Recall that what you are going through has been, and is being, experienced by others, so you are not alone. You are in covenant with others who care and are experiencing inner darkness.
- And above all, let your faith remind you that God is walking beside you as you are now traveling a very different journey.

They often ask, "Will all this remove the pain?" And I tell them truthfully, "No. Nothing can do that."

Which prompts them to then ask, with a sense of resignation and frustration, what the use of this is.

THE ART OF KINDNESS

In response, I remind them that if you must experience such sadness—and there is no way to recapture your loss or undo what has happened—such steps will open you to a new way of appreciating your life in a way that others who have not walked through such darkness can ever know. And that is certainly worth the effort!

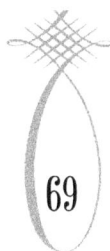

69

Spiritual and Psychological Carbon Monoxide Poisoning

Some people experience physical, psychological, and even spiritual trauma when they are young. Knowing what we now know from the psychological post-traumatic growth and the spirituality of suffering literature, some can deepen as people in ways that would not have been possible had they not faced such early deprivations or horrors. Consequently, they turn out to be the most compassionate people. Such people amaze and inspire me to become more gracious and giving myself.

There are others who struggle to make a good life for themselves—in their family and interpersonal relationships—despite what happened to them.

Finally, there is a smaller but quite toxic group of people who unconsciously spend their lives continually demanding that others make up for their past losses while always worrying that they are losing something or being taken advantage of. Consequently, their relationships—including their own children and friends—become psychologically and spiritually drained in their efforts not to disappoint these people, because they know that their early losses were real and only want to make life better for them. (I have seen this especially in the case of treating adult children of parents, who have experienced horrible circumstances.)

THE ART OF KINDNESS

This is sad for those who are continually being reminded that they are not doing enough, but it is also a loss for the suffering individuals. Constantly, they miss the simple joy of freely giving to others because they are so focused on themselves; they are unconsciously believing that life was horrible once and now permanently owes them.

There is also a particular danger for professional and non-professional helpers and healers who work with such suffering and demanding souls. I remind them that, when they are treating such persons, they must make sure of their diagnosis before they determine the treatment. Otherwise, the helper will become discouraged and the person suffering will only be burdened by expectations that they will not understand, they will mistakenly feel unappreciated for the past pain they have endured, and they will become angry because they want others to change and agree with them.

One of the major sources of this *"spiritual carbon monoxide poisoning,"* where compassionate people are silently drained of their own positive spirit by contact with negative hurting individuals, can occur when someone close to them has unconsciously decided to remain needy and not understood. However, when this occurs, even though they don't do it on purpose, or at least not maliciously, the helping people need to recognize that if others inadvertently hurt them, it still hurts!

So, the answer, here, is to psychologically move your heads by doing such things as:

- Remaining present, if you can, but lowering expectations of the person and your ability to meet their demands.
- If possible, let them know that you recognize they have been hurt in the past, but *they* need to change if they are to get more out of life.
- Ensure that you have other people in your life who are healthier and can both receive and give to you without expecting anything in return.

Spiritual and Psychological Carbon Monoxide Poisoning

- Appreciate that this type of person's demanding style of behavior is often more advanced and manipulative than your own ability to be present without losing your own sense of self-appreciation and self-respect. Again and again, some people can convince you that you haven't given them what they want, in the way they want it, when they want it, and because of this, you feel bad. When this happens, respect the needy person's powerful manipulative abilities and laugh at yourself when you begin to feel guilty again. Indeed, laughter at yourself is good medicine.

The Challenge of Transition

Some people keep looking back at the "good ol' days" that also hid some horrible realities, while others totally condemn the past while missing the real good that was truly there—no matter how bad it might have been.

Instead, we are called to find the good from the past and leave behind what was bad. This lets us as individuals and as a society to be more open, discerning, hopeful, and courageous to recognize, embrace, and change now.

Leaving our former psychological home empty-handed is unnecessary. On the one hand, our own and the world's history contain valuable wisdom. On the other hand, being on the journey to the next destination without a new map will only leave us adrift in spiritual nostalgia.

People who see things in black and white may exist comfortably for a while; that is the temptation. Whereas those who are willing to entertain ambiguities truly live; that is the gift. During our short time on this earth, the choice, at any given phase of our life, is ours.

Swiss psychiatrist, Carl Jung, wanted us to recognize the dangerous temptation of hiding ourselves mentally. He is claimed to have noted: "Thinking is difficult. That's why most people judge." To this I would add: When we judge, we often do so with insufficient information—not simply about others but about faith, God, and ourselves.

The Challenge of Transition

One of the most common mistakes made by counselors, spiritual directors/guides, medical professionals, social workers, and neighborhood organizers is that they don't question people and situations enough before deciding on a course of action. The same can be said about how we face ourselves, our faith, and the world, today. In striving to be content, we miss so much that is good and necessary to understand in ourselves and our dynamic situations—especially during the challenge of transition.

When we were very young, we may have thought that hiding under the covers would save us. It is understandable that we would think that as children. However, to do so as adults, is another story—especially when we label those covers "faith," "religion," "values," and fail to read sacred scripture carefully, and reflect on the life Jesus.

When we ask, "What would Jesus do?" we are being asked in return by Jesus, "Never mind. What are *you* going to do?" If our answer—not simply in words but actions—doesn't contain the true love that may make our present psychological world uncomfortable, we may be temporarily deluding ourselves but, in the end, we are not fooling God even if we are using religious words.

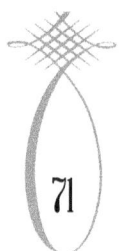

Our Gifts and Growth

I was supervising a pastoral counseling student, who asked me what my central charism (gift) is as a therapist and mentor. After some reflection, I told her that it is having the spirit of being a failure.

My response was not what she expected and caught her totally off guard. After she regained her composure, she then wanted to know more and whether being a failure could be something good.

I needed to figure out how to explain what I meant. Finally, I said, "All my life, I have been very attuned to my failures with a memory that would hear praise in a whisper and criticism as thunder. This, as you might expect, was a problem for me growing up, especially in my teens, until I realized that this psychological music and dysfunctional thinking could be of great spiritual benefit as an individual and as a therapist."

The student now looked really puzzled, so I continued, "By feeling like a failure, I could be more sensitive at times than some of my colleagues, when my patients were going through periods of anxiety, alienation, and feeling a sense of failure. I was also in a better position to truly understand people from a different culture, gender, or sexual orientation, when they expressed feelings of not measuring up or 'knowing their place' according to society or even within their own religious denomination or church community.

"So, while I still share with patients how to cognitively dispute dysfunctional thoughts and beliefs that are exaggerated or false, I also have a daily spiritual exercise using sacred scripture to remind me that my name is written on the hands of God. As Trappist monk, Thomas Merton, is said to have taught: 'You don't have to worry about a public image or even an ideal image when you are a friend of God.'"

The student finally responded that feeling like a failure certainly must still be a cross, especially when looking at past mistakes in life.

I said, "Yes, it can be very tough, at times. No one likes to feel a failure or experience the sharpness of a real or perceived past mistake in life. Darkness, however, need not be the final word in our lives. If we look at failure correctly, it can be the first word in a new, more healthy perspective, as well as a psychological and spiritual door to greater sensitivity toward others who are going through dark periods. Most important, failure is an essential reminder that with God's love and our humility to see both our gifts and growth with a sense of equanimity, following the cross, there is always the resurrection."

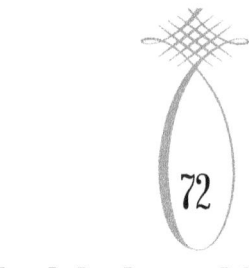

Meditative Moments

For some people, bustling activities can block out the vision or music of life. That is not the case if we can see the broader picture for ourselves in life. For this to happen, we need to check our life's flow so that we don't end up like so many others who suddenly realize that they have had a busy life, but not a full one.

When we take out a few moments each day in silence, solitude, and gratitude, we are very fortunate because we can then listen to the music of our lives. This music can be heard at any age so it doesn't matter how old we are when we begin experiencing it anew. We can only be alive in the moment. Moreover, in meditative moments, we realize that "negative nostalgia"—looking back and focusing on what we have missed—is a waste of time.

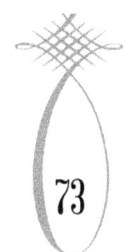

The Circle of Grace

I used to visit my favorite florist often because I love to decorate the inside of my house with fresh beauty. Most times, I would see this young girl behind the counter with a dour look until one day a boy she was obviously interested in showed up and instantly brought a broad smile to her face. The look transformed her!

It was amazing how someone could have this sudden positive impact on a person. Now, looking back, I think I should also—in word, deed, and presence—strive to be such a person for those I meet. Of course, this goal is unattainable, but it is certainly worthy to have a compassionate attitude that helps others find a heart in them that smiles as well. If I do this, instead of primarily seeking others to feel sorry for, protect, or encourage me, no matter the response I receive, I can enter an amazing circle of grace and, in some way, allow God to touch me as well. I know this for a fact, because I have experienced it many times.

74

God's Emanating Love

Years ago, when I was speaking at Seton Hall University, Cardinal Basil Hume, Archbishop of Westminster, England, was also giving a presentation and shared a story. He said that when he was very young, he loved cookies. The problem was that the cookie jar was under a small painting of the Sacred Heart of Jesus. And so, he felt guilty every time he took a cookie.

Later in life, when he shared the story with a fellow priest, his friend said that he also had a picture of the Sacred Heart in his house but instead saw it as a sign of God's emanating love.

After hearing that, Cardinal Hume said to his friend, "I am sorry I didn't feel that way back then. If I did, I would have taken two cookies!"

A Gentle Presence

I look around me and pray:

- Help me with my negative thoughts that aren't helpful and are often not true.
- Let me see my feelings as portals to understanding how I view life so that I can grow.
- Make my actions align with the compassionate nature I have been given but sometimes don't practice.
- Help me to honor this day that may be my last and should be marked by generosity and allow me to walk in the Garden as my "grandparents" did before me at the start of time.
- Help me to listen more deeply to the Spirit of Truth, instead of merely hearing the world's rumblings, so that I will come to know a gentle presence. What more can I ask for today than that?

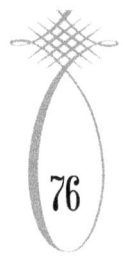

76

The Ripple Effect

As the deaths of beautiful children and a teacher—society's symbol of nurture—are vivid in my mind, I am reminded of a horrific scene in Texas.

When speaking to the Texas Medical Association Alliance, the audience was the spouses of physicians who silently carry many burdens and are often the unrecognized victims of healthcare. They not only keep the home fires burning but do so much more in ways that people don't see or appreciate. Yet, they continue!

I also gave the keynote address in Denver at an annual conference for eight hundred ministers. They also had the experience of going to schools to support the mothers, fathers, and siblings of dead children who were mourning and asked why? *Why did this happen to my small, defenseless child?*

While we are shocked that a disturbed and angry person would cowardly kill the helpless and future of America, there are those who, in the face of such darkness, still refuse to bow to this discouragement, the final home of the ego, but see it, rather, as an even stronger impetus to "act justly, love mercy, and walk humbly with your God" (see Mic 6:8).

Discouragement only feeds into the hands of self-serving politicians and leaders who would have us do nothing. As I recall the sound of children dying and screaming in fear, I know that is not an option. Instead, like the members of the Texas Medical Association Alliance, ministers, teachers, and other caregivers facing darkness

The Ripple Effect

with a sense of faithfulness, we must see what actions in life will strengthen our society and stand against divisiveness that leads to such horrors and then *do something*—no matter how small. Kindness and faithfulness to what we believe is good have a ripple effect. Let's start making ripples.

Memorial Day

One of my joys is meeting people who have given so much for others. Sometimes, in a moment of candor or an off-handed remark, they reveal the faces of others who often remain in the shadows but have also given so much.

I was once speaking with a chaplain, who had spent most of his ministry in the military, about the joys and sadness of his role. At one point, he spoke about the impact not only on him but his family as well. He commented that, after he retired, he asked one of his sons how tough it was on him being a child of a military chaplain.

The boy, who was now an adult with children of his own, said, "You weren't there, Dad. When we had important events in our life, you rarely could come. I know it wasn't your fault, but it still hurt."

The spouses and children of those in the military as well as those in medicine, nursing, ministry, and the other helping professions, pay a price for the service of their spouses and parents. They sit in the shadows and their sacrifice often remains unrecognized, even though the cost may be high and the memories tough—very tough.

On Memorial Day, I remember those who have made the ultimate sacrifice and recall those in their families and circles of friends who have also paid a dear price. This is a day to shine the light on all those who support military members and those in other caring professions. There is a good deal of sacrifice and generosity that we don't see. In a world where horrible acts and words seem to

Memorial Day

be in such sharp relief, I see such love—and there is plenty of it to see when we look into the shadows of those who served others so completely. Love is at the heart of life. God is Love. Memorial Day reminds me of this, and I need such memories not only to recall the sacrifice of others, but to continue to uphold me as well.

Openness and Compassion

On the Fourth of July, I am reminded of my visit to Europe to speak at a large U.S. Air Force base to airmen and members of NATO's Intelligence Fusion Center. One of my goals is always to put people at ease so they feel free to share their concerns and views. This is especially so in the case of people native to those countries as well as those from America who are visiting or working there.

During one of these visits, feelings concerning the U.S. president who was in office at the time were negative. More than once I would hear about his lack of concern for, or knowledge about the world at large, as well as his lack of protection of the environment and his general arrogance. People who are nationalistic and feel "my country right or wrong" might bristle when people from other lands say something negative about our president or criticize America. Whereas, true patriots know their country is not perfect and must remain open to criticism so that we can do all we can to make it better and contribute to the greater community—*our* world.

The same is true of us as people. First, we need to know our God-given strengths and gifts. Not to do so deprives not only us but also the wider community of our contribution of compassionate service to others. Moreover, if we are religious, it is a slap in God's face not to acknowledge these talents and to nurture and share them with others. After all, why were we given them?

We also need to see those instances when we ignore our "growing edges"—those defensive elements within us—and deny

Openness and Compassion

our shortcomings/sins or the egotistical exaggerations of our very talents—being boastful rather than enjoying and sharing our gifts with humility.

As a nation and as individuals, we must hold in one hand our talents and our troublesome qualities in the other. Such clarity and balance allow us to continue to grow psychologically and spiritually. Honoring the complete picture of our country and ourselves—both accurately positive and negative—can lead to an indescribable fullness. However, if we want to get a real indication of what this looks like, we must seek to embrace true humility, and take steps to inspire people through openness and compassion. If we do this, we will experience ourselves and our nation with the sense of real liberty, justice, and freedom for all that the founders of our democracy intended.

Holy Selfishness

Just because I use religious words, it doesn't mean that what I say or the judgments I make and the actions I take are spiritually correct. Instead, they may actually be merely moral justifications for my inordinate fears and selfishness. When I think that I am embracing simplicity and faithfulness to the truth, it may well be simplistic thinking that can encourage divisiveness and hate of what and who I find challenging. Consequently, it is not only dangerous for me but also for those who look to me for guidance.

Therefore, I need to pray for the humility to not do harm in saying and doing what I feel is for the greater good. When my words and actions are divisive, it often means that I need to spend more time alone with God. Rather than sitting with my own ego trying to be secure in the status quo, I need to embrace a dynamic, living God requesting me to change, be more open, and not hide behind the cross to remain spiritually alive.

80

Silence and Solitude

When COVID-19 first hit, and people were restricted to their homes, they often had to encounter unfamiliar longer periods of silence. If we are not used to quieting our souls and being open to the voice of God, silence can be a challenge. One reason for this is that, emotionally, silence creates a psychological vacuum. And, as many of us were taught in high school science class, nature abhors vacuums. Therefore, such empty spaces are filled with the voice of our preconscious.

Since the preconscious includes what is lying just beyond our awareness—those unacceptable things that we have pushed down and avoided—we may find such an awareness disturbing. It may lead to thoughts in which we blame others, accuse ourselves, or become discouraged because we, or the world, hasn't changed to our liking. However, if we greet any unpleasant thoughts that arise with a spirit of intrigue and the knowledge that God loves us no matter what, silence and solitude can become our friends and teachers.

Moreover, during these reflections, we will find ourselves more deeply honoring the African proverb: "A wise man fills his brain before emptying his mouth." And so, others will be grateful that we pray and don't immediately react in hurtful ways. When we pray, we also set the stage for a greater gap between the stimuli we receive and the responses we make. Some suggest that this result is an increase in our emotional intelligence; others might call it grace. While some of us simply call it *beautiful*.

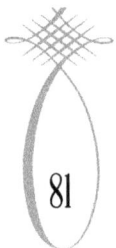

81

Invisible Connections

As people age, they often comment on a radical change in their interpersonal networks and come to see themselves as more invisible to family and friends.

Here, they are usually referring to children who have moved away or are so involved in raising their own families that they are not in touch as often. They are also indicating that the friends they have had in the past are now involved with other people, work, or have moved geographically, either diminishing or eliminating contact.

It is at these times when people need to be more in tune with their new "invisible connections." These are very different from their past relationships. For instance, since they are not as actively involved with people, in general, time for silence and solitude naturally becomes an option. Becoming aware of how to honor rather than waste this time is good. This can be done by reading books or listening to music or podcasts, and even attending lectures on mindfulness, silence, solitude, and prayer.

It is important to be more sensitive to old or new acquaintances who suddenly reach out. We often find that they may now be more available and appreciative of a return email than others who were at our sides in the past.

The new space that comes as we get older also allows us to interact more graciously with people that we pass in the neighborhood, supermarket, or meet online. We also have time to meet peo-

Invisible Connections

ple more regularly and to read scripture, novels, biographies, and poetry.

Nevertheless, one must let go of a past style, previous expectations, and ways of fulfilling our interpersonal needs, and be open to a new phase of life. Otherwise, we are like the persons who move to Arizona bringing with them green plants from the northeast of America to reproduce what they left behind, instead of opening their eyes to value, among other things, the stunning red rocks and sunsets of the Southwest. Just as the physical desert they have entered will blossom for them, so can an interpersonal one for us. We need to unveil the invisible connections that are there and be open to the new gifts, and not fail to see them because they weren't what we had.

Similarly, I recall people whom I've hurt and felt guilty about because I was wrong in my estimation of them. Now, I see them as better people and, rather than being the object of my complaints, they have grown in my estimation. I wonder if I would feel the same about myself if I took a closer look.

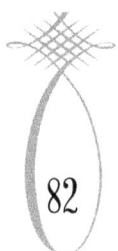

Seeing More Clearly

Some memories remain because they offer us a surprising lesson in life. For me, one of these memories was of a simple occurrence when I was speaking in Guatemala to people responsible for the spiritual care of an indigenous group that had been tortured and abused.

I was taking a break in the flourishing town of Antigua. The beauty of this village is amazing. Around noon, my guide suggested that we have lunch and indicated that we would be taking lunch "right here."

I was confused since there was no restaurant anywhere in sight. At which point, he walked over to a wall covered with ivy, reached over, turned a knob, and opened a door. Beyond it was an open area with a mariachi band playing, a woman cooking tortillas on a grill, and people speaking animatedly as they ate their meals. I was stunned. If you didn't know the restaurant was there you would miss it.

This is what happens when we are too focused on our own world. We can walk past the opportunity to find new wisdom, peace, and joy, because we can't see the door.

With eyes that see more clearly, we can also see further. Amid "the ivy of entitlement, righteousness, and other defenses hiding the way," we see the possibility to live more deeply in ways that would not have been possible before—and those eyes are ones of love.

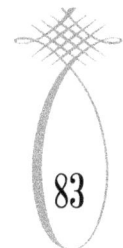

Walking Gently Together

Often during the holidays, there are those who have lost someone or are suffering in some way, and the brightness of the festive time can have the opposite effect on them. One of my students, who was also a minister, once told me that he didn't think so much sadness could fit into his body.

When you sense such a reaction, walk gently with the person, because you may be the only one who is able to understand. This is crucial, because as American author, professor, feminist, and social activist, bell hooks once said: "Rarely, if ever, are any of us healed in isolation. Healing is an act of communion."

84

Embracing Impermanence

On one of those rare occasions when I have been ill, the symptoms lasted for almost a week. During that time, I encountered some psychological feelings that surprised me. I felt discouraged and lonely. I recalled the contemplative Thomas Merton saying about a similar time when he lay in bed in the monastery infirmary, and after getting over the discomfort of being sick, he saw the period as an invitation to have prolonged quiet time with God. It was a chance for both of us not simply to be ill but to discover!

Fortunately, this memory gave me a chance to relax with God and live in the present more intentionally. After all, there was nowhere else to go! One of the gifts of this period of illness was a clearer recognition of impermanence—our vulnerability to sickness and death. Such an insight can change one's values and lifestyle.

This illness helped me to appreciate more clearly and personally the powerful parable of Jesus that applies to all of us who are preoccupied with security and the future:

> Then he told them a parable: "The land of a rich man produced abundantly. And he thought to himself, 'What should I do, for I have no place to store my crops?' Then he said, 'I will do this: I will pull down my barns and build larger ones, and there I will store all my grain and my goods. And I will say to my soul, Soul, you have ample goods laid up for many years; relax, eat, drink, be

Embracing Impermanence

merry.' But God said to him, 'You fool! This very night your life is being demanded of you. And the things you have prepared, whose will they be?' So it is with those who store up treasures for themselves but are not rich toward God." (Luke 12:16–21)

Similarly, the simple and profound Vietnamese Buddhist monk, Thich Nhat Hanh, reminds us: "Impermanence does not necessarily lead to suffering. What makes us suffer is wanting things to be permanent when they are not."

As I reflected on the words of Jesus, Merton, and Thich Nhat Hanh, the sense of understanding impermanence provided me with a chance to have my soul softened so that I could have a different perspective on life. Should I plan for the future? Of course. However, being preoccupied with it in a way that misses the now and assumes we will be here forever is foolish. There is no absolute security, no guarantee, except in God.

This grace and the freedom of being in touch with impermanence—that we will all *definitely* die—brought a sense of ease to might have once been a very disturbing reality. And so, I decided to take this experience to prayer, each morning, every day, without fail, because it is easy to rationalize your impermanence and not honor it, even though you think you are in touch with your mortality.

I had an aunt who, when I would ask her if she was going to a wedding that was a few months off, would normally reply, "Oh, I don't even know if I will be alive then." However, if I asked her what she was doing the next day, she provided me with a complete schedule of activities. There was no doubt that she would be here tomorrow. But, on one tomorrow, she would not be there.

I wonder if she was surprised at that moment of her death. I know I don't want to be. I want to be present for it and grateful for all those who have been in my life whom I know wished me well and those whom I never realized quietly supported and appreciated me. I want to be present to all the ordinary gifts of the world—the quiet forest, the crashing waves of the sea, the endless plains and deserts, and even the excited bustle of the cities.

Of course no one wants to be ill; death can be frightening. But knowing that our lives are fleeting opens the door to the reality of impermanence so the present moment now becomes precious—so very, very precious. And so, with this awareness in our hearts, we can treat others and ourselves with more kindness and understanding. Why be hurtful and ungracious to someone who may die today?

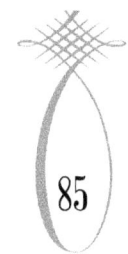

Two Different Women

The first woman was financially wealthy, yet she also possessed anger, competition, and disdain. Men and women who rode with her in the elevator would notice her physical beauty, "What gorgeous clothes! She's so lucky!" But what they didn't see was that she also silently wore bitterness, loneliness, and a "no-one-understands" attitude. Additionally, they didn't see the invisible dangers the woman had never feared and faced growing up. She believed—then as now—that a wonderful life only grows outside of oneself. Consequently, when she got what she wanted, when she wanted it, and how she wanted it, she was happy for a while—though not too happy because she didn't want others to feel that she was OK and stop feeding her what she felt she deserved.

    The second woman was quite different. She was simply clad and would sit on a bench in the park with her dog at her feet. The dog would look at me in a way that said, "Don't even think of sitting down if you don't have a treat for me." After giving him one, he'd wag his tail back and forth as if to say, "Atta boy! You did well. There's hope for you!" The woman would smile at me, gaze at the trees, and look at me with an expression that seemed to ask, "Do you like the park that I don't own? Do you know in your heart that simple kindness to others also makes your own world better? Will you borrow my gratitude and make it your own? Will you seek to have a healthy perspective even if the world says you are poor and

THE ART OF KINDNESS

not a worldly success? After leaving, will you share such joy with others so that they might have greater peace, too?"

After standing up and leaving with a final farewell, I would walk around the park feeling strong enough to sit again with the other woman. I could do this again because I now had the spirit that the woman on the bench had shared with me. But I was also very puzzled because, as soon as the woman on the bench had given so much to me, a resupply of what is important in life seemed to return to her. I knew this for a fact because as I looked back, I could see it in her facial expression as she met the next lucky person who greeted her and was also quietly blessed.

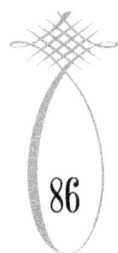

Some Life Lessons

Persons who enter psychotherapy or spiritual mentoring or direction do so for many specific reasons. If they remain in the relationship long enough, they usually learn several broad life lessons like the following:

- The self is limited so don't waste energy on what and who you can't control even if (and this is important) your goals are worthy.
- Do what you can and let others and God take care of the residue.
- You are not in the success business. You are in the *faithfulness* business.
- Time in silence, solitude, and gratitude is not a luxury or only to be had when there is nothing else to do. Such periods are the center of life because they allow us to reflect, be appreciative, unlearn what is no longer helpful and become more intrigued about ourselves and the world.
- Self-blame may feel like we are being honest with ourselves. Projecting blame onto others may seem like we are only saying what is true. Both are a waste of valuable time in life.

THE ART OF KINDNESS

- Some people like to watch life as if it were a movie; others truly want to live their lives. Decide which one you are.
- Most people act as if they are going to live forever, even if they say they know they are going to die "someday" in the future, but not today or tomorrow, of course. You must learn that your time—and the time of those you love—is brief. Once we know this, we will tend to be kinder, discern what is truly important, and even in doing our daily chores, mindfully, prayerfully not rush to our graves doing "good and necessary things."
- When we blame others for our misfortune it is fun but, in giving away the blame, we also give away the power to be happy now, in this world. It is like when someone misbehaves by cutting us off on the highway and we reward his misbehavior by getting angry, letting our blood pressure rise, and destroying the joy of our journey. Some may say that this is natural, but it is time to be unnatural and free.
- If you are unhappy with yourself, it is often because your behavior is simply an exaggeration of your gifts. For instance, if you are the type of person who people take advantage of, you don't want to give up being kind—we have enough selfish people in this world. Instead, you need to prune your graciousness, so you don't let people psychologically step on you or spiritually abuse you while you still remain helpful to those in need. Don't punish others for the bad behavior of a few.
- There are three phases in life that need to be honored: Most of our lives are finding out who we are and then sharing this charism/gift with others while enjoying being that type of person. The second phase is to prune that gift so that it blossoms rather than becom-

ing a caricature. So, if you are a listener, you must speak up at times. If you are passionate, you don't need to always fill the room with yourself. The final phase is to focus on your "pruning element" until you die. And so, if you are a passionate person like me and need to prune that element with gentleness, you focus on gentleness.
- You must not only focus on the "lyrics" of life—what you should do in certain situations—as important as this is. The "music"—how we approach situations (our attitude or perspective)—is even more important.

These are but several themes from therapy and spiritual guidance. I try to remember them myself. Do I ever fail to live them out? Oh, of course! But I use such failures as a reminder to laugh at the thought that I could ever do them perfectly and approach the whole journey with intrigue. After all, it is the only life I have, so why not get a kick out of it, generously share it with others, and let God take care of the residue? (It is amazing how we often want to do God's job—very insulting to the Divine.)

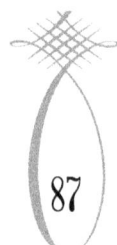

Faith and Respect

A woman shared that she was worried about her son's behavior. When I asked her how old he was, she said, "Fifty." I questioned whether he had always behaved this way or whether it was a change from when he was small. She replied that he was always this way and that it had always upset her.

Looking puzzled, I asked, "So, you are still looking at your son now at the age of fifty, waiting for him to change?" "Yes," she said, "because I know he can do better."

"Ah, well we can remove your worry easily."

"Really?" she responded surprised.

"Yes, each time you look at your fifty-year-old son and worry about him because you want him to change, you need only do two things. First, focus on the positive traits he has and the wonderful ways he expresses those gifts. Second, have faith that other good people in his life and God will encourage him to share those very talents even more completely."

"And, if I do that, he will change?"

"No, *you* will change. Each time you do those two things, *you* will feel relieved."

Undaunted, she pursued the topic further, "Well, how will I be guaranteed that he will also change because of others and God?"

I was amazed at her tenacity and responded, "That is why letting go and letting God act directly and through others is called *faith*, and that simultaneously honoring your son for who he already

Faith and Respect

is in so many positive ways is known as *respect*, because he is, after all, *imago Dei*."

Try this technique each time you start to worry. Do it for a month and then return and we shall see if an adjustment needs to be made to what I have recommended. Letting go and letting God are two very powerful approaches but sometimes need a booster or slight adjustment in focus.

Healing

When people have lost someone very close to them, their world is shattered. Those around them also feel totally lost—often because they want them to feel better, the past to return, and the loss to be erased. But it can't be erased. It is horrible, unchangeable, and permanent.

Psychological and spiritual guides know this. They don't varnish it. Instead, they let the person slowly tell stories about the person who is gone. They are patient when others want the person to move on. But timing is everything. Recognition that the loss will never be undone is clear.

So, what can be done? Some say that time heals all. Psychologists have a less romantic notion and understand that new intervening variables help those living with the loss in the best way possible.

Listening

Most people are willing to offer advice.
Others are willing to remain quiet,
While waiting for their opportunity
to speak.

True listening
is an entirely different matter,
for it requires more than
attention to words.

It requires respect,
opens the door for emotions to be shared,
and provides freedom,
so that others can openly be themselves.

Listening is a consultation of the heart.

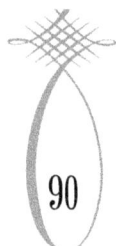

Different Beautiful Gifts

New situations are natural teachers, *if* we let them play that role. Sometimes, though, unless we get a "wisdom-nudge" and embrace it, new learning is missed or refused.

A very small boy from a rural area of central Africa was brought by an uncle to the west coast for the first time. His face broke into a smile, and he shouted with joy when he saw ocean waves, because he had never encountered them before.

At the end of the day, his uncle said, "We must go now." The young boy's face dropped, and he pleaded, "Can't we at least wait until the waves stop?"

His uncle smiled and responded, "The ocean is not like a lake—even a large one. The large waves never stop here like the ripples in the lake near our home. This is a new lesson for you to learn: Do not be disappointed in our lake because it remains calm. Yet, still rejoice in the constant energy of this ocean you are meeting for the first time.

"They are different from each other. In being so, they share different beautiful gifts."

The Lighthouse

My family goes to the beach together each summer for one week. We go either to Bethany Beach in Delaware or to Stone Harbor in New Jersey. It is a time when we relax together and renew our relationships in ways that are not possible when gathering for only an event or even a visit lasting several days.

Each summer reminds me of an interaction I had years ago with a brilliant psychiatrist and clinical supervisor in my doctoral training program at Hahnemann Medical College and Hospital in Philadelphia. Of all the classes, lessons, and psychotherapeutic techniques, this interaction guides me not only in my clinical work but also in my personal life.

This training analyst possessed not only great wisdom but also a wonderful attitude. During our last session, I took the initiative, courage really, to mention that he had taught me a great deal to interact with an array of personalities and intervene with a broad range of psychological problems. However, what struck me the most about our interactions was his sense of presence, not simply with me but toward life. That was something that I really wanted to take from him, not only into my clinical work but through the rest of my life.

His response was simple and took the form of a story. He said, "Although I have been blessed with a good disposition and parents who had personalities that allowed me to nurture mine even further, a terrible event that happened in my own family served as a 'lighthouse' whenever I entered turbulent psychological seas in my own life."

THE ART OF KINDNESS

"What happened was that we were at the beach, and my son suddenly became very ill. He was a college student at the time and had a chronic disease. While away during his junior year, where we had little contact with him, he stopped attending to it for reasons that are too complex to explain here. As a result, the following summer, when we were in Virginia Beach for a vacation, he became sick. He was on the edge of going into a coma before we realized how severe it was, and then took him to the hospital. He just made it in time and is now a very happy and productive person. Like his mother, my wife, he has great vision, creativity, and commitment. If this had happened while he was at university that year, he probably wouldn't have been discovered in time and would have died."

"This event woke me up to the fragility of life—even for the very young whom we are close to and who make life such a joy for us. And so, anytime I get lost, I consciously recall this event and three important realizations."

"First, I appreciate anew the fragility of life and what is truly important and so regain a healthy perspective. Second, I recognize my own limits, so I do what I can to help myself and others deal with the challenges that arise, and then surrender the rest to others and let God take care of it. Finally, I seek to let go and truly become grateful once again for life—my own and those whom I love dearly."

This important interaction with a wise supervisor more than forty years ago continues to help me appreciate the fragility and pure gift of life. It remains the one factor that changes life for the good forever. It is my permanent psychological and spiritual lighthouse, especially in turbulent, emotional waters. It helps me gain, regain, and maintain a healthy perspective no matter what is happening. When we embrace the impermanence of life, all is changed for the better every day that we, and those we love, are alive.

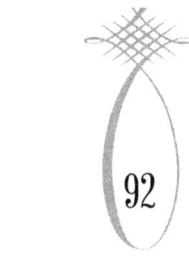

Positive Prophets

A woman once shared with me her depression over the sad things happening in the world and noted that, while these things are a reality, she didn't want to stick her head in the sand and be guilty of denial. I waited a moment before offering her a new, and quite challenging, paradoxical perspective, "Yes, we don't want to be ignorant of the pain in the world or within our own lives. However, we must also realize that if we attend solely and inordinately to darkness, it will become unnecessarily larger than it needs to be and even take up the space needed for something else that is more profound and true."

I reminded her that it is important to remember the very real presence of love, graciousness, compassion, peace, and joy in the world. While we don't want to fool ourselves about the darkness, we also don't want to play down all that is good in the world. We need to look at them both but especially at the love and goodness. By doing this we will then increase our perception of what reflects God's loving presence. Consequently, our attitude will be reformed, our inner peace will increase, and our compassion toward others and our desire to act in helpful ways to become more present not out of duty or desperation, but naturally, will grow. We will want to feel God's love and peace within us and share that caring presence with others. In focusing on God's presence, we are open to the miracle.

Looking puzzled, she asked, "What miracle?" In response, I noted that peace and joy will grow so much in our hearts that they will not lose their way in a tunnel of despair. Instead, they will find their outlet in a spirit of faithfulness to what is good in us and make the world a better place for others. As a result, we will increase the good we can do when people need it the most. We will become "positive prophets." Through prayer God invites us "to be *my light* in the world *now*." I hope you can feel this call as well.

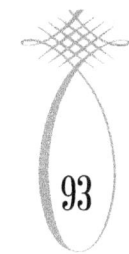

The Gifts of Clarity

Recently, I saw a hurtful post about Pope Francis and was saddened that people sometimes mistake their own rigidity and anxiety about uncertainty for being a faithful religious person. But there was a broader lesson here for me. When I avoid seeing my own psychological anxieties or don't want to face the uncertainties in life or embrace the challenges of a dynamic faith, I live in an envelope of illusion. I may feel more comfortable and "spiritually smug," but it prevents me from truly learning from those who challenge me to be more open and ends in mindless or self-serving behavior that often hurts others. When I am open to God's call to change, I experience my faith and life in new, wonderful ways.

It is not easy, but it is simple when I have a living faith born of being reflective, loving, and open every day. This helps me keep my fingers on the pulse of my anxiety and anger so I can stop and then check on the cognitions—the ways of thinking, perceiving and understanding—I have about a situation that are producing these unpleasant feelings so that my responses become more healthy and healing. Moreover, such an attitude is rewarded by the gifts of new creativity, a greater spirit of hope, and a more intriguing sense of God and my faith rather than what I have imagined. These are but some of the gifts of clarity.

So, the negative post about Pope Francis didn't end in sadness for me, after all. It reminded me of God's call to "be not afraid" so that I can see new light in a sometimes dark and psychologically defended world. Rather than running from the pope's call to love and be inclusive, I can respond positively and not condemn others for their anxiety, but seek to serve rather than throw stones and build walls around the life I have constructed for myself because of my own unrecognized insecurities.

These goals are impossible if I try to do them on my own. Still, failing will only help me remember God's grace and the prayer of others like you to enable me to persist, be patient, and have faith.

94

Good Friendship

Some friends ask you how you are doing, and this is fine; others ask but are also interested in doing what they can to help.

Knowing the difference between these two types of friends causes less personal disappointment and doesn't burden others with what they cannot do because of their own limits or needs.

Remember the wise saying from Anthony de Mello in his book, *One Minute Wisdom*: "Don't try to teach a cow to sing. It frustrates the teacher and irritates the heck out of the cow."

95

Enjoying Life

A devout woman came to me because she didn't seem to be enjoying the closing years of her life and became upset when her son and daughter weren't grateful for, or didn't follow, her suggestions. Although her sessions with me were helpful, I knew that I needed to include the spiritual element to have a real impact. One day, I commented that she seemed very religious yet found it strange that she seemed to lack a certain type of prayerful attitude. She responded that she did think of herself as a person of prayer but was interested to know what type of prayerful attitude she lacked.

My response was in the form of a story: "If you give a young woman a gift at Christmas, what would be the best way of her thanking you? Well, she could say 'thank you' and that would be lovely. However, an even better sign of gratitude would be seeing the person really enjoying the gift herself and freely sharing it with others while expecting nothing in return."

To fully enjoy life is like smiling at God in thanksgiving for the gift of our birth. But having a willingness to share that life with others with no need for thanks, or receiving the results we want, is an even broader embrace of God's gift of life. Furthermore, at this time when much of the world and many families are experiencing darkness, sharing the peace in our hearts that such a spiritual atti-

Enjoying Life

tude spawns, can be a torch in the night for those who need it most in our families, neighborhoods, and lives. They may not mention it when we do this, but some day, it may be the positive memory they need to go on, and God will certainly notice, and smile.

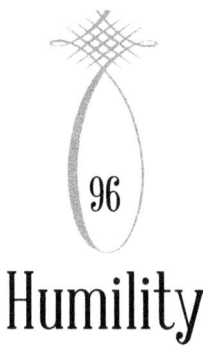

Humility

I feel helpless around some people because they are convinced that they don't need help.

Sages have cautioned people throughout the ages not to offer advice unless it is requested. This makes sense, although I have always found it hard to stand by while someone could be helped with more knowledge even though they seem to enjoy being cemented in a particular view—even to the extent of repeating it firmly when challenged, as if doing this provided proof of its veracity.

Sometimes, a rule must be broken when a single theme arises that is so important to share, especially when it is a quiet danger that can hurt a person, their work, and even their family if they continue to hold to it.

Some people think that it is what they don't know that will hurt them and, of course, this is true to an extent. However, an even greater danger is what we think we already know but really don't.

Humility is key in uncovering and addressing this danger, because when we take humility and add it to knowledge, we get wisdom. It is from such wisdom that a beautiful life deepens and shines a light for others.

We shouldn't be afraid to learn. I know that it may hurt our pride at times. Yet, it will also open the window to the spiritual air we need to breathe during these times of challenge and change.

Regardless, I bow to reality, knowing that it is all right to feel helpless around certain people because they feel they don't need

Humility

help. I now understand better the saying that "ignorance is bliss." Unfortunately, though, the price for such comfort is that nothing new, and possibly necessary, is allowed to grow and flourish.

Reflecting on this theme reminds me that I, as "the helper," sometimes want to save others from the quiet dangers of life and believe that I have all the answers. Ultimately, I need humility as well and must tread gently. My assumptions need to continually be examined!

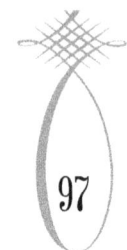

97

The Countryside of Compassion

When a woman came to me years ago for her weekly psychotherapy session, her facial expression was unusual. After she sat down, I waited for her to share the words behind her look.

Finally, she shared that two interactions had taken her by surprise the previous week. The first was that she learned that her sister had cancer and needed to make a change in her work schedule. She called one of her colleagues at home to inform her. She had never called this person at home before, *ever*! The colleague was very abrupt because her family was visiting and they were on the way out to dine, and never acknowledged the severity of what she was sharing. The second interaction occurred after one of her children came down with the flu. Her closest neighbors knew because they spoke while she was heading to the pharmacy to fulfill a prescription for her child. A few days later, they saw each other while she was watering her outdoor plants, but they never even asked how her child was doing.

After sharing this, she stopped for a few moments as if she were thinking further about these recent events. Now, one of the key goals of psychotherapy is to be comfortable enough with silence so that the person can have the opportunity to explore what they are thinking, understanding, and perceiving more deeply.

The Countryside of Compassion

Finally, she added, "I guess that is why psychotherapy, counseling, and ministry can be so powerful. You truly do put the other person first. You get out of yourself and seek to be a torch during those twilight times of confusion, loneliness, and rejection that people experience."

Today, many people are self-involved, angry, take offense easily, feel unappreciated, and seek only groups that will agree with them. However, like professionals in mental health and ministry, if we step out of our own small world, focus compassionately on others, and maintain a healthy self-compassion, the negative spell that many people now seem to be under can be broken. In bringing a spiritual and psychological torch to others by attending carefully to what they are saying, thinking, and feeling, our world also opens up. We encounter the beautiful landscape of peace and joy that mark the "countryside of compassion." We are no longer confined to the psychological and spiritual sickbed of being overly self-involved and bound by our own fears, needs, and agendas. Moreover, we also become freer to enjoy the many gifts that God has already given us because true compassion is a circle of grace, in which all benefit.

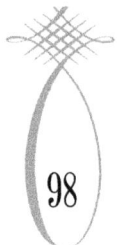

Invisible Darkness

I recall once trying to hear my patient tell me about her life, but it was difficult because the psychiatrist in the next office was laughing so loud.

After this happened, I asked the psychiatrist, "What the heck were you doing in there? The laughter was uproarious."

He responded kindly saying, "Sorry I disrupted your session. The patient I had in there is from show business and he is one of the funniest people I have ever met and told him so."

"How did he respond?" I asked.

He said, "Well, I am not here to entertain you."

"What did you say to that?"

"Well," he said, "I asked him, 'Then, why are you doing it?'"

For some people, every Tuesday seems like the dark night of the soul. They are always expressing how tough life is for them and that style is really the best they can do. Unfortunately, it has the opposite effect because they can't be grateful for life and, in the process, drain the rest of their families who are constantly trying to make life better for them and, in the process, they lose their sense of joy.

There are other people, however, who you would never know are experiencing depression, anxiety, loneliness, alienation, and loss. They are such lively, caring spirits, and the only time you see their pain is when they have no energy left to hide it.

One of the benefits of them seeing a therapist is that they feel less of a need to ensure their darkness is invisible, but even with me,

Invisible Darkness

they would often apologize when their sadness and loneliness was revealed. I would often respond by looking around the room and saying, "Ah, someone took the sign down."

They would look puzzled and ask, "What sign?" To which I would respond, "The one that says it is OK to cry here," and they would often nod their heads, laugh, and say something to the effect of, "If only people knew all the energy that I am expending to keep it all together."

"Invisible darkness" is more common than most people think. It is important for those of us who are caregivers or good neighbors to listen, encourage, and be open to signs that people are stumbling. Similarly, if we are quietly troubled when people do reach out to us, we must feel free to share our sense of loss, alienation, and darkness. If we carefully choose the people in our lives, we will get some support that wasn't there before, and it will help us not simply survive but also have the energy to learn more deeply about ourselves and the true values of life that only tough times can teach.

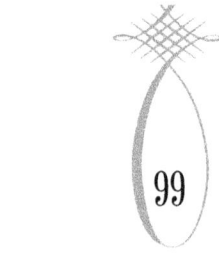

99

Our Hidden Mental Compartments

When people come to me for mentoring, one of the goals is to help them open the psychological compartments that are hidden from their own conscious minds. This is essential because their lack of awareness of these areas can be spiritually crippling. This isn't easy because some people are very at ease with themselves and their style so it wouldn't occur to them to question themselves. They are overconfident on the path they are walking, and you can sense it in how they share and post their feelings, thoughts, and opinions. Yet, as the American author Joseph Campbell once quipped, "If the path before you is clear, you're probably on someone else's."

There are always new things for us to fathom—especially when we have strong feelings or are strongly convinced of something.

Powerful Spaces

There is a hurt in the world
that is true and must be honored.
Times in one's family and among friends
and neighbors that can be tough.
But there are also powerful spaces
in the dark that bring light...
and these should not be ignored
but embraced for the joy and peace
they offer us
so we can smile and enjoy
knowing
we are not alone...
but loved
by the One who matters.
Don't miss them.

About the Author

For over forty-five years, Dr. Robert Wicks has been called upon to bring calm into chaos by individuals and groups experiencing stress, anxiety, and confusion. He has spoken on his major areas of expertise—resilience, self-care, the prevention of *secondary* stress (the pressures encountered in reaching out to others), and the integration of psychology and classic spirituality—to members of Congress and their chiefs of staff on Capitol Hill; led a course in resilience in Beirut for relief workers brought there from Aleppo, Syria, for a conference with him; and presented at Johns Hopkins School of Medicine, the U.S. Air Force Academy, the Mayo Clinic, the North American Aerospace Defense Command, the Defense Intelligence Agency, as well as at Boston's Children's Hospital, Harvard Divinity School, Yale School of Nursing, Princeton Theological Seminary, and to members of the NATO Intelligence Fusion Center in England. He has also spoken at the Boston Public Library's commemoration of the Boston Marathon bombing, addressed ten thousand educators in the Air Canada Arena in Toronto, spoken to the U.S. Army Medical Command, was the opening keynote speaker to 1,500 physicians for the American Medical Directors Association, spoken at the FBI and New York City Police Academies, and addressed caregivers in twenty different countries including: China, Vietnam, India, Thailand, Haiti, Northern Ireland, Hungary, Guatemala, Malta, New Zealand, Australia, France, England, and South Africa.

Dr. Wicks received his doctorate in psychology from Hahnemann Medical College and Hospital, is professor emeritus at Loyola University Maryland, and has taught in universities and professional schools of psychology, medicine, nursing, theology, education, and social work. In 2003, he was the commencement speaker for Wright State School of Medicine in Dayton, Ohio, and in 2005, he was both a visiting scholar and the commencement speaker at Stritch School of Medicine in Chicago. He was also commencement speaker at, and the recipient of honorary doctorates from, Georgian Court, Caldwell, and Marywood Universities.

In 1994, he was responsible for the psychological debriefing of NGOs/relief workers evacuated from Rwanda during that country's genocide. In 1993, and again in 2001, he worked in Cambodia with professionals from the English-speaking community who were present to help the Khmer people rebuild their nation following years of terror and torture. In 2006, he delivered presentations on self-care at the National Naval Medical Center in Bethesda, Maryland, and the Walter Reed Army Hospital to those health-care professionals responsible for Iraq and Afghan war veterans. More recently, he addressed U.S. Army health-care professionals returning from Africa where they were assisting during the Ebola crisis.

Dr. Wicks has published more than fifty books for both professionals and the public, including the bestselling *Riding the Dragon* that has sold more than seventy thousand copies. His latest books include: *Quiet Dangers, Do You Have a Moment?, The Simple Care of a Hopeful Heart*, and the second edition of *Bounce: Living the Resilient Life*. His professional books include *Overcoming Secondary Stress in Medical and Nursing Practice* (second edition with Gloria Donnelly), *The Resilient Clinician* (second edition with Mary Beth Werdel), and *The Inner Life of the Counselor*. He is also the coauthor of *A Primer on Posttraumatic Growth* and senior coeditor of *Clinician's Guide to Self-Renewal*. Dr. Wicks has received the first annual Alumni Award for Excellence in Professional Psychology from Widener University and is the recipient of the Humanitarian of the Year Award from the American Counseling Association's Division on Spirituality, Ethics and Religious Values in Counseling.

Other Books by Robert J. Wicks

Everyday Simplicity: A Practical Guide to Spiritual Growth (2000)

Living a Gentle, Passionate Life (2000)

Simple Changes: Quietly Overcoming Barriers to Personal and Professional Growth (2000)

Touching the Holy: Ordinariness, Self-Esteem, and Friendship (2007)

Crossing the Desert: Learning to Let Go, See Clearly, and Live Simply (2008)

Prayerfulness: Awakening to the Fullness of Life (2009)

The Inner Life of the Counselor (2012)

A Primer on Posttraumatic Growth: An Introduction and Guide [Co-author with Mary Beth Werdel] (2012)

No Problem: Turning the Next Corner in the Spiritual Life (2014)

Perspective: The Calm within the Storm (2014)

Availability: The Challenge and the Gift of Being Present (2015)

Night Call: Embracing Compassion and Hope in a Troubled World (2017)

The Tao of Ordinariness: Humility and Simplicity in a Narcissistic Age (2019)

Heartstorming: Creating a Place God Can Call Home (2020)

THE ART OF KINDNESS

Overcoming Secondary Stress in Medical and Nursing Practice
[Second Edition with Gloria Donnelly] (2021)

Prayers for Uncertain Times (2021)

The Simple Care of a Hopeful Heart: Mentoring Yourself in Difficult Times (2021)

Do You Have a Moment?: Spiritual Posts to Open and Close the Day (2022)

Riding the Dragon: 10 Lessons for Inner Strength in Challenging Times
[Twentieth Anniversary Edition] (2022)

Bounce: Living the Resilient Life [Second Edition] (2023)

Let's Look Together: Henri Nouwen as Spiritual Mentor (2023)

Quiet Dangers: Navigating the Psychological Challenges of Spiritual Intimacy (2023)

The Resilient Clinician
[Second Edition with Mary Beth Werdel] (2023)

Praise for Other Books

Bounce: Living the Resilient Life (2009/2023)
"Insightful, practical, and often humorous, *Bounce* is the right tonic for the spirit we need in a stressful world."
~ Helen Prejean, author of *Dead Man Walking*

Riding the Dragon: 10 Lessons for Inner Strength in Challenging Times (2003/2022)
"Compassionate and wise."
~ Jack Kornfield, author of *A Path with Heart*

The Tao of Ordinariness: Humility and Simplicity in a Narcissistic Age (2019)
"This is a welcome recipe as many of us struggle with ambiguity, uncertainty and the pressures of modern life."
~ Patricia Davidson, PhD, dean, Johns Hopkins School of Nursing

Night Call: Embracing Compassion and Hope in a Troubled World (2017)
"A renowned psychologist and specialist in the area of resilience, has written a truly impressive book."
~ Robert Brooks, PhD, co-author of *The Power of Resilience*

Perspective: The Calm within the Storm (2014)
"This is the kind of book you can't put down because it is so necessary."
~ Alexandra Fuller, author of *New York Times* bestselling book *Cocktail Hour Under the Tree of Forgetfulness*

THE ART OF KINDNESS

Crossing the Desert: Learning to Let Go,
See Clearly, and Live Simply (2008)
"…a wonderous guide for those who wish to transform
their lives today."
~ Kathleen Kennedy Townsend,
former lieutenant governor of Maryland